HOW TO IMPROVE READING COMPREHENSION QUICKLY BY KNOWING YOUR PERSONAL READING COMPREHENSION STYLE

QUICK, EASY TIPS TO IMPROVE COMPREHENSION THROUGH THE BRAIN'S FASTEST SUPERLINKS LEARNING STYLE

RICKI LINKSMAN

HOW TO IMPROVE READING COMPREHENSION QUICKLY BY KNOWING YOUR PERSONAL READING COMPREHENSION STYLE

QUICK, EASY TIPS TO IMPROVE COMPREHENSION THROUGH THE BRAIN'S FASTEST SUPERLINKS LEARNING STYLE

HOW TO IMPROVE READING COMPREHENSION
QUICKLY BY KNOWING YOUR PERSONAL READING
COMPREHENSION STYLE
Copyright © 1996-2016 Ricki Linksman

This edition published 2016 by National Reading
Diagnostics Institute, Naperville, IL
ISBN: 978-1-928997-93-1

Praise for Ricki Linksman's Books and Brain-Based Learning Methods

From Publications:

From "Woman News," New York, New York:

"There is a way to learn anything you want rapidly and successfully. The technique can be applied to any sort of learning in any field you choose. Each of us has a Superlink— the easiest method for us to fully learn information. Once you've found your Superlink, you can use it to learn in ways that are easy, effortless, and automatic." —published in an article in New York's "Woman News" called, "Mind Power: Smarten Up! Tap into Your Brain's Superlink—Learning Becomes Easy, Effortless, and Automatic"

From "L.A. Parent" and "San Diego Parent," California:

"All children in California will be reading at grade level or above by the end of third grade.' With this promise, California state leaders have made reading instruction in the early grades (K through Grade 3) a top priority in the public schools. So while the politicians are trying to do their part, how can parents help their little readers measure up? According to Ricki Linksman, author of *Your Child Can Be a Great Reader*, parents should first figure out their child's learning style.

i

"Research shows that each of us receives information in different ways. Visual learners learn best through their eyes, auditory learners through their ears, tactile learners by touching, and kinesthetic learners by moving around."

–From an article in the "L.A. Times" and "San Diego Times," called "What is Your Child's Reading Style? If You Know How Your Child Reads You Can Help Him/Her Learn," by Judy Molland

Family Time Magazine:
Feb. 2007, published an article about how Keys to Reading Success™ helped two local suburban Chicago area schools (Fairmont and East Aurora) meet state standards.

From the Iowa "Gazette," Cedar Rapids, Iowa:
"Author Ricki Linksman has plenty of tips for parents who want to be sure their kids love to read, and can read well."

From the "Abilene Reporter-News," Abilene, Texas:
"This step-by-step guide is designed to help children overcome every kind of reading problem and get back up to grade level or beyond. It is filled with short, fun activities to do at home and provides pointers to boost self-esteem and motivation." (Jan. 24, 1999)

From a Public School District Superintendent:

"Ricki Linksman has synthesized the educational research into concepts which makes learning accessible to anyone. While the term differentiation of instruction is very popular in the world of education, Ricki Linksman provides concrete examples and techniques of combining learning styles with brain hemispheric preference to create an individualized "superlink." These techniques are personalized to open the pathways for anyone to learn anything quickly. For example, our junior high school went from 2/3 of the students below state level on state reading assessment tests to 2/3 of the students above state level in reading within eight months."

−Dr. Michael Early, Public School District Superintendent, Illinois, and former School Principal in West Suburban Chicago

From a School Superintendent:

"This is the only reading program I have found with the scientifically-based reading research that has proven statistics to raise reading levels so rapidly. Keys to Reading Success™ helped our school get off the state watch list that it had been on for 6 years, and this year—2006—we have finally made AYP or met state reading standards by using the program for only 6 months. The discipline problems in our school have been dramatically reduced as students went from reading below grade level to reading above grade level within 6 months. They are engaged in learning and have raised their self-esteem and motivation to achieve in school. Its parent involvement lessons in all learning styles and brain styles allow parents and teachers to work as a team for every child's success. This program ensures that every student can raise reading levels and test scores by Keys to Reading Success's™ comprehensive but easy-to-use reading diagnosis, learning styles and brain styles assessment, and its powerful, effective, and engaging teacher reading lesson plans in all learning styles. Using learning styles has helped every student learn to read in his or her most effective and fastest learning style possible."

–Dr. Doris Langon, Superintendent,
Fairmont District 89, Lockport, Illinois.

From a District School Superintendent on Gains in High School, Middle School, and Elementary School, including Indian Oaks Academy for Special Needs:

"Through using this program, significant gains were made in our district in elementary, middle, and high school on the CTBS (Cognitive Test of Basic Skills) test. Our ISAT (Illinois Standards Achievement Test) scores in reading showed significant growth. Gains in reading ranged from 1-8 grade levels in 9 months in the elementary, middle, and high school grades. From 86%-99% of students in grades 1-5 accelerated to read from 1-8 years above grade level in reading within 9 months (including Regular Ed and Special Ed students). In the middle school, students rose from 1-6 years above grade level. In the high school 99.5% of students grades 9-12 rose from 1-2 grade levels in reading in 9 months."

–M.S., Asst. Supt. Curriculum, Manteno School District

From a Principal of a Charter School in East Los Angeles, California:

"East Los Angeles school, Culture and Language Academy of Success (CLAS), a charter school devoted to African-American culture in the Los Angeles Unified School District rose from not meeting State Standards in reading to exceeding state standards in reading in 1 year using Ricki Linksman's *Keys to Reading Success* program using the techniques in *How to Learn Anything Quickly*. On a scale from 200-1000, they reached 773, with 35 points gain, and came close to the 800 superior school status. LA Unified District only reached 600 with a 9 point gain in 1 year. CLAS achieved 773, while California's state average was 635."

–Principal, Dr. Sharroky Hollie,
CLAS Charter School, Los Angeles, California

From a School Principal at Dieterich School in District 131, East Aurora, Illinois:

"With 83% of the school population speaking only Spanish and being enrolled in the English Language Learners (ELL) program, Dieterich School in East Aurora, Illinois, scored as the third highest in the district in their reading scores on the March 2006 ISAT Illinois State Achievement Test) reading test using Keys to Reading Success™ and Superlinks to Accelerated Learning™, using techniques from *How to Learn Anything Quickly*."

–Principal, Dieterich Elementary School,
East Aurora, Illinois

From an Elementary School:
"2/3 of the students in grades 1-3 rose from 1-7 grade levels in reading above grade level in one school year."

–M.S., Teacher, Elementary School in Joliet, Illinois

From a Technology Director:
"We need to get past the assembly line way we teach and test. Through the use of technology and the Keys to Reading Success program, teachers can easily manage "progressive monitoring," diagnostic testing and reporting for students on an individual basis. This in turn allows teachers to customize each student's learning needs...what could be better?"

-Vicki Dewitt, Technology Hub Director,
Edwardsville, Illinois

From Learning Identity, South Africa:
"Ricki Linksman has a heart to make a difference in the lives of those who struggle with reading. She has developed a unique learning and reading program based on brain

processing and learning styles, which undertakes to teach ANYONE how to read and learn and most importantly how to comprehend the content matter. We have had remarkable success with 100's of students utilizing Ricki's Keys to Reading Success and Superlinks to Accelerated Learning program, and consider it an honor to be a part of her work."

–Trish Gatland, Learning Identity, South Africa

From Sports Coaches and Trainers:

From a Head Football Coach:

"Using these accelerated learning techniques such as teaching through learning styles has helped our university football team have its first winning season ever. The athletes learned the plays faster and better through these techniques. We also had our best academic year ever, for our academic support to our athletes."

–Ken Karcher, University Head Football Coach

From a Graduate of the National Academy of Sports Medicine (NASM) Certified Personal Trainer program:

"I passed the National Academy of Sports Medicine (NASM) Certified Personal Trainer (CPT) exam. The NASM CPT is considered the Cadillac of certifications for Personal Fitness Trainers and the exam has a notoriously high failure rate. The course itself (almost all correspondence based) is exceptionally detailed oriented and requires students to learn everything from intricate human anatomy to psychology, and everything in between. If I had known how hard it was going to be when I set out to do it, I don't think I would have even attempted it! While not all certifications are equal, those who have done the NASM CPT course and passed are in my opinion, border level scientists. Having done it myself, my respect level has gone through the roof not just for other NASM Certified Personal Trainers but also for myself. I wanted to let you know how grateful I am to you for all you did for me in learning about myself, my learning style (highly kinesthetic) and how to work around potential roadblocks. I have since learned even more about what makes me "tick." It's an exciting journey! Ricki, I wanted to take the time out to thank you from the bottom of my heart for everything you did for me--I don't think any of my success would have been possible without your help and expertise."

–Skye Middleton, NASM Certified Personal Trainer

From Teachers Who Took the Master's Degree Teacher Education Superlinks Courses:

"In that one year, I learned more about teaching reading than from my entire college education."

–M.S., Teacher, Farragut Elementary School, Joliet, Illinois

"The teacher training in reading is the best I have ever taken."

"The course in how to teach reading stretched my thinking about learning. The material was practical, hands-on, and relevant. Excellent trainer. It is the best course I have taken in years."

"I now have some tools and tests to evaluate why some of my students are not learning and to have techniques to teach to all my students. I recommend that every teacher take this training--it will open your eyes and hearts."

From Adult Learners:

"I am 26 years old and throughout my school career was labeled dyslexic. I never learned to read and ended up with a job and career that did not interest me. I wanted to go to college. Within 6 months of using Ricki Linksman's accelerated learning techniques, I learned to read well enough to pass the college entrance examination, and have been admitted to a college that will prepare me for the career I want."

"I am in my 50's and could never read. Through the Superlinks learning style and brain style test, I discovered that I had never been able to learn to read before because the method used in the school when I was growing up did not match the way I needed to learn. Working with Ricki Linksman and her accelerated learning techniques, I learned how to read in my best learning style and I can now enjoy books. Ricki then donated her services for free to our local branch of the *Literacy Volunteer of America* to train tutors in her Keys to Reading Success™ reading comprehension and memory program so they could keep working with adults who wanted to learn to read."

–J.S., Chicago

I had purchased Ricki's earlier book, *How to Learn Anything Quickly: Quick, Easy Tips to Improve Memory, Reading Comprehension, Test-Taking Skills, and Learning through the Brain's Fastest Superlinks Learning Style* a year ago when I was starting a study-at-home Medical Transcription program. At first, I somehow did not get past the first two pages. It ended up tucked in the bottom of my nightstand drawer. (I am a tactile-mixed with left-side dominate learner). Three weeks ago after struggling with comprehension and memory, I bit the bullet and got an extension. But, more importantly, I decided to commit to reading the book. Wow, I am glad I picked it up and forced myself to push past the first few pages. I have not been able to put it down, and will be finishing it up today. It was a really eye opening to see that the teaching styles of my teachers varied in my primary, elementary, high school, and college experiences. I passed Biology and Psychology with flying colors, but could not seem to get a passing grade from Nutrition class. Of course with your confidence shattered, you never see the parallels. You never look at the classes you did pass and wonder what went wrong; you just give up. (Or label yourself). How sobering to know that it was not my lack of ability; it was the learning style in which the information was presented—that each teacher had his or her own way of presenting the material, and it was the teachers that taught closer to my learning style where I excelled the most. I have a renewed commitment to complete my at-home study course and will take all that I have learned in this book with me throughout my life, for every subject I wish to learn. I have also bought two more copies for my husband and sister. This letter is just a huge thank you for writing such an easy to understand book, full of knowledge that can change anyone who is curious how to improve their learning and memory. Thank you!

–D.H., adult learner

From a Title 1 Success Story:
A 1st grader was not reading on level by mid-first grade. The parents and teachers were so concerned that they wanted to do an evaluation to see if he had a learning disability. During the waiting period for his evaluation, the Keys to Reading Success Accelerated Phonics Program was used with him in

his Title 1 class. It was discovered that he was a kinesthetic learner. He used the kinesthetic component of the Keys to Reading Success Accelerated Phonics Program, and within months, mastered all the phonetic patterns and was not only able to read well at a 1st grade level, but accelerated into 2nd grade level reading, while still a first grader. By the time he was evaluated by the psychologist, they discovered he actually had an I.Q. in the 140's and he was then placed in a gifted program. Had we not discovered his learning style and taught him through that method, he may have fallen even further behind in his reading level and it may have taken years to find out that he did not have a learning disability.

From University Instructors:
"Every teacher should use Keys to Reading Success. It is the most complete program of reading available. It is an excellent training tool for new teachers."

–College Instructor for Graduate Education Courses for Teachers, Benedictine University, Lisle, Illinois

From Parents Who Used the Superlinks Methods with Their Children and Teens:
"My high school son was getting D's and F's, but after a reading diagnosis and learning style assessment from Keys to Reading Success and receiving instruction in study skills and memory skills in his learning style, he is now getting A's. The program has also helped him on his SATs and ACTs."

–M.O., Parent, Naperville, Illinois

"When we started coming to Ricki Linksman at National Reading Diagnostics Institute, my son was in first grade, but reading at a kindergarten level, and his self-confidence was down. After working with Ricki for the past 11 months using her Keys to Reading Success™, Superlinks to Accelerated Learning™, and Off the Wall Phonics™ program, his reading level has improved so much that he is wanting to read books and complete Accelerated Reader™ book tests at school. My son is enjoying reading now that he reads at grade level and we will continue to work with Ricki to get him past grade level. What a difference! Even his teacher in school has noticed and commented, 'He is to be commended for reading and taking tests on 23 books this quarter! He's starting to enjoy reading, which is wonderful.'"

**–L.M., Wheaton Christian Grammar School,
Winfield, Illinois**

"My child has made tremendous gains in a short time. His self-esteem has risen dramatically."

–A.P, Parent, Naperville

"My 10th grade son went from grades of 'F's" and 'D's' to 'A's' in 4 weeks. His study skills, comprehension, and memory has improved tremendously."

–Parent, Westmont

"In 6 months, my 4th grade child, who was reading 3 years below level, came up to grade level and is doing well in school."

–Parent, Lisle

"I have learned so much about how to help my son and about learning styles in general. I have to say that the frustration level when doing homework or reading has gone down dramatically.

–M.H., Chicago

"We have seen improved results in my son's tests and overall academics. In fact, he made the honor roll!! I appreciate the fact she is able to see how he best comprehends his reading material and incorporates the best plan for him. We are very happy to see his overall comprehension improve and especially his confidence. Thank you Ricki!"

–L.Z., parent

"My kindergartener is now reading 3rd grade books, and doing addition, subtraction, multiplication, and division over several months' time."

–Mr. R.M., Parent, Naperville

"For the first time, my 2nd grader could read on his grade level, and his self-esteem has increased tremendously."

–Parent, Chicago

"We wanted our 4-year-old child to qualify for a gifted school but she didn't achieve the necessary score on her first test. Within less than a year, she not only learned to read at a 3rd grade level, but was able to qualify for the gifted school. We are so thrilled with the results."

–S.D., Parent, Wheaton

"I home school my children and I learned how to accelerate their reading at home."

–Parent, Batavia

"My gifted child loves the challenging activities."

–Parent, Downers Grove

"I've looked for years for help for my son and Ricki Linksman is the only person that came through. My son has made more progress in these last 8 months than he has K through 6th grade. She provides concrete solutions to his specific areas that he needs help in. I recommend Ricki's book to anyone whose child is struggling at school or who wants to give their child an advantage to succeed. Ricki has not only helped my son to learn but his attitude and confidence has increased dramatically. I have seen amazing results for my son. Not only has his reading level improved dramatically but his confidence and enthusiasm are through the roof!"

–S.S, Parent, Illinois

"If you are reading this, you are probably concerned about the progress your child or grandchild is making in learning to read. I was in the same position several years ago. My grandson wasn't learning to read in his school. He had been left back in the same grade twice because he could not read. He was diagnosed with ADD and a learning disability. We spent years trying to find out why he could not read because he was a bright boy. As a concerned parent or grandparent, I got on the Internet and found Ricki Linksman's National Reading Diagnostics Institute and its Keys to Reading Success® and its Superlinks to Accelerated Learning™ programs which determined what his learning style and brain hemispheric preference was. The assessment determined he was a kinesthetic and tactile learner with a right brain hemispheric preference. It gave us a prescriptive plan to solve the problem and lessons in his best learning style. Within the first lesson of Keys to Reading Success®, using kinesthetic right brain learning techniques, my grandson read for the first time in his life, to his joy and excitement. After only one session with the Keys to Reading Success® materials, I watched this little guy read solid first-grade material that he had never been able to read before for the first time in his life. Yet, several hours before that first session, he had not even known the letters of the alphabet. I almost fell out of my chair, I was so excited. I knew then that I was on the right track, and I had found the right person and right techniques and program to teach this young lad how to read. He has been reading ever since. Within a few months, he was able to read at his grade level, and we were able to take him off his ADD medication. We now know what works for him and we attributed it to National Reading Diagnostics Institute and Keys to Reading Success. The developer of Keys to Reading Success®, Ricki Linksman, is truly the Michael Jordan of reading."

–Rusty Acree, Concerned Grandparent, Retd. Naval Officer, and Field Judge for University Football Games, Richmond, Virginia

And from his grandson, who wrote: When asked about what he liked best about his trip to Chicago, the lad wrote: "Learning to read. Thank you, Mrs. Linksman."

"Our teenager did not score well on the practice test for a high school entrance exam to Benet Academy, a college preparatory school. After a few months of work at National Reading Diagnostics Institute, areas of need were targeted and our teen got 99% on the actual entrance exam and was admitted to the preparatory school."

–Parent, Lisle

"Our son was in special education classes since 1st grade and by 7th grade still had not learned to read. We brought him to Ricki Linksman for a reading diagnosis and she gave him a Keys to Reading Success® reading diagnostic test, Superlinks™ learning style and brain style test, and tutoring instruction.

Our son learned to read in months and no longer needed to be in special education. His self-esteem has gone up and he is so happy now."

–B. Burke., Parent, Miami, Florida

"My high school sophomore never dropped below A's or B's before, so when he dropped to a C in English, we were beside ourselves with frustration. After using these strategies for only 6 weeks, he not only went back up to A, but was the only student in the class to receive a writing award!"

–M.H., Parent

"We did not feel our middle school son had the skills to be ready for high school. He was struggling in many of his school subjects and even needed audios to read his assigned books to him. After only two months using these strategies, he can now read by himself, and his grades have improved to the point where the principal and teachers are astounded by his amazing progress! He feels proud of himself, enjoys school now, and has boosted his vocabulary, memory, study skills, and test-taking skills. The best part is that he does not need to be read to, but can read at and above his grade level all by himself!

–K.A, Parent

"My daughter struggled with reading in early elementary school, and I realized that when she read to me, she was only memorizing the book and could not read on her own. Ricki Linksman at National Reading Diagnostics Institute gave the Superlinks test and found out she was a kinesthetic right brain learner and the techniques in her school were not matching how she best learned. By using kinesthetic right brain techniques for her learning. Ricki not only taught her to read at grade level within a few months, but raised her several years above her age as well. Throughout the rest of her school career, she became a top reader and student in her class, no longer needed tutoring, and ended up in honors classes. In high school, she was number eleven in overall standing in her school. She returned to National Reading Diagnostics Institute to work with Ricki Linksman for ACT test prep, in her kinesthetic right brain learning style, and got a perfect score on the English ACT! She not only gained admission to numerous universities, but she was offered several scholarships, won academic awards, and ended up selecting a college, whose scholarship is paying $25,000.00 a year for each of the four years for her tuition. We are so glad we found National Reading Diagnostics Institute and Ricki Linksman and recommend her to any parent who wants to lay the foundation early for their child's future success in high school, college, and in life."

–J.O., Parent, Wheaton, Illinois

Awards and Achievements:

IASCD (Illinois Association for Supervision and Curriculum Development) awarded a WINN Research Certificate of Award of Merit for Outstanding Research to Ricki Linksman, Developer of Keys to Reading Success, for "Maximizing Reading Growth in Nine Months from 2-5 Grade Levels by Using Accelerated Phonics Taught through Learning Styles."

OTHER BOOKS AND RESOURCES
BY THE AUTHOR, RICKI LINKSMAN

Books, eBooks, and Software about the Brain; Memory Improvement; Accelerated Learning through Learning Styles and Brain Styles; Kinesthetic, Tactile, Visual, Auditory Left and Right Brain Learners; Reading and Listening Comprehension Strategies; Accelerated Phonics; Vocabulary; Test-taking, Note-taking, and Study Skills and Test Prep for High School and College Entrance Exams, (ACT, SAT); Self-Esteem; Motivation; Concentration; and Focus

How to Learn Anything Quickly: Quick, Easy Tips to Improve Memory, Reading Comprehension, Test-Taking Skills, and Learning through the Brain's Fastest Superlinks Learning Style

How to Improve Memory Quickly: Quick, Easy Tips to Improve Memory through the Brain's Fastest Superlinks Learning Style

The Fine Line between ADHD and Kinesthetic Learners: 197 Kinesthetic Activities to Quickly Improve Reading, Memory, and Learning in Just 10 Weeks: The Ultimate Parent Guide to ADD, ADHD, and Kinesthetic Learners

How to Improve Reading Comprehension Quickly by Knowing Your Personal Reading Comprehension Style: Quick, Easy Tips to Improve Comprehension through the Brain's Fastest Superlinks Learning Style

Solving Your Child's Reading Problem

From ADHD or ADD to A's: Improve Reading, Memory, and Learning Quickly for Kinesthetic Learners

Your Child Can Be a Great Reader

Keys to Reading Success™: Internet Reading Program (includes Linksman Passage Reading Tests, Linksman Phonics Diagnostic Test, and Superlinks Assessment, plus 1000s of pages of reading lesson plans in all learning styles: Kinesthetic, Tactile, Visual, and Auditory with adaptations for right and left brain learners in reading comprehension, phonics, vocabulary, test-taking strategies, test prep, and study skills.

Superlinks to Accelerated Learning Assessment™ (includes Linksman Learning Style Preference Assessment™ and Linksman Brain Hemispheric Preference Assessment™)

Off the Wall Phonics (Accelerated K-12, College, and Adult

Phonics Program to Improve Reading Comprehension, Word Reading and Fluency for Kinesthetic, Tactile, Visual, and Auditory Learners, both Right Brain and Left Brain Learners)

Kinesthetic Vocabulary Activities Your Child Will Love

Tactile Vocabulary Activities Your Child Will Love

How to Quickly Improve Memory and Learning for Kinesthetic Left and Right Brain Superlinks Learning Styles

How to Quickly Improve Memory and Learning for Tactile Left and Right Brain Superlinks Learning Styles

How to Quickly Improve Memory and Learning for Visual Left and Right Brain Superlinks Learning Styles

How to Quickly Improve Memory and Learning for Auditory Left and Right Brain Superlinks Learning Styles

How to Quickly Improve Reading Comprehension for Kinesthetic Left and Right Brain Superlinks Learning Styles

How to Quickly Improve Reading Comprehension for Tactile Left and Right Brain Superlinks Learning Styles

For other products, books, eBooks, software, trainings, and e-courses visit:

www.readinginstruction.com
www.keyslearning.com
www.superlinkslearning.com
www.keystoreadingsuccesss.com
or e-mail: info@keyslearning.com

Dedicated to

all those who devote their lives
to helping others be all they can in life.

TABLE OF CONTENTS

INTRODUCTION

You can improve your reading comprehension to remember *everything* you read and learn quickly.

Applying brain research to teaching people how to improve their reading comprehension for the past thirty years, people of all ages, have used these quick, easy and fun tips and strategies to achieve success in the shortest possible time. Whether you want to use your memory power for school, college, job, career, sports, or hobbies, you can become a memory whiz. You do not have to wait for months or years to learn these secrets to improving memory quickly—they are available now within this book for anyone to use to learn anything for any purpose.

When I published my book, *How to Learn Anything Quickly: Quick, Easy Tips to Improve Memory, Reading Comprehension, and Test-taking Skills through the Brain's Fastest Superlinks Learning Style,* many people asked me if I could just do a book focused only on reading comprehension, especially for adults who aim to keep their reading comprehension skills active and strong as they age. Others felt they wanted a simple handbook to help them with challenges such as learning a new job or going back to school. Coaches, professors, teachers, and trainers also want techniques to help those they are teaching or training accelerate their speed of comprehending the material. I decided to publish this short handbook focused on reading comprehension with quick, easy strategies anyone can use. If you want to extend your memory power for reading comprehension, study and note-taking, and test-taking skills and to use it for learning any

1

subject, you will find these extended topics in the full compendium on the subject: *How to Learn Anything Quickly: Quick, Easy Tips to Improve Memory, Reading Comprehension, and Test-taking Skills through the Brain's Fastest Superlinks Learning Style.*

After using and testing these revolutionary brain- based memory methods for decades with corporations, businesses, sports teams, universities, colleges, elementary, middle, and high school districts, and with individuals, students, parents, and families, I have tracked how these strategies have consistently proven to take any learner to success within days, weeks, and months—not years! Now, I share with you in this book those same quick, easy tips to increase your reading comprehension to learn anything quickly. Use your brain's energy powers to succeed in the competitive job market, whether to get hired for a job, keep your job, or keep pace with new information and technology in a rapidly changing job market. *How to Improve Reading Comprehension Quickly by Knowing Your Personal Reading Comprehension Style* gives you fast, simple, and powerful reading comprehension strategies to comprehend *everything* you read and learn for rapid success.

Since the 1970s, I have applied brain-based teaching methods to help people of all ages (pre-K, kindergarten, grades 1-12, college, and adult) use their brain's unique Superlinks learning style and brain style to improve reading comprehension quickly and successfully. These powerful techniques, proven for over 35 years in school districts, colleges, corporations, businesses, and sports teams have helped people become top students and workers in the shortest possible time.

Among those who have been successful using these memory techniques are:

- Adult learners from college to post-graduate school to raise grades and improve reading comprehension, vocabulary, note taking, study skills, and test-taking skills
- Baby-boomers and seniors to exercise their brain and comprehension for lifelong learning
- Adults in the job market needing to rapidly learn new information and skills to find or keep a job, pass certification tests, start a new career when downsized, or keep pace with rapidly changing technology in the workplace
- Parents to help their child or teen (pre-K, kindergarten, grades 1- 12, or college, whether in regular education, special education, gifted, honors, bilingual, ESL, ELL, dual language, Title 1, or Remedial Reading programs, or who have ADHD or ADD) improve reading comprehension concentration, focus, and self-esteem, and raise grades, reading levels, and test scores for state or standardized tests or high school or college placement tests (i.e., ACT or SAT) in the shortest possible time.
- Teachers, college instructors, coaches, or trainers to teach students or trainees in their fastest Superlinks learning style and brain style for mastery
- Doctors, psychologists, psychiatrists, social workers, and therapists to give clients tools to reduce stress-related illnesses from fear of school or test taking by giving them confidence to learn and comprehend anything

- Football, baseball, basketball, soccer, hockey, or golf coaches who want their athletes to rapidly learn and memorize their sports playbook or skills and keep up academic grades
- Spanish-speaking students or those who speak any other language to rapidly learn English, or English-speaking students who want to know how to learn and comprehend any language quickly
- Anyone wanting to improve relationships and communication skills with family, spouses, significant others, friends, or co-workers or employees, whether a visual, auditory, tactile, kinesthetic, or left-brain or right- brain learner to understand themselves and others and how they comprehend information.

It has been heart-warming and rewarding to receive feedback from people of all ages throughout the world that these simple, easy methods to increase reading comprehension have transformed their lives by helping them achieve success in any field—quickly. My hope is that all readers of this book, *How to Improve Reading Comprehension Quickly: Quick, Easy Tips to Improve Comprehension by Knowing Your Personal Reading Comprehension Style,* unlock your own amazing brain power, experience the joy of learning, raise your confidence and self-esteem, and help you attain success starting right now in whatever area you wish to achieve in life!

–Ricki Linksman

PART 1:
INCREASE READING COMPREHENSION
THROUGH BRAIN-BASED METHODS

CHAPTER 1:
HOW TO IMPROVE YOUR READING COMPREHENSION QUICKLY

Do you want to keep your comprehension sharp? Are you concerned whether your reading comprehension will stay strong as you become older? Do you wish to increase your reading comprehension to learn any subject quickly? Are you a job seeker or employee looking for a new job and must learn how to learn and comprehend new information fast? Do you need to improve your reading comprehension to learn study skills, note taking, and test-taking skills to prepare for a career certification test, college boards, or placement exam but it has been such a long time since you last used these skills in school that you need a quick refresher? Do you find it hard to keep up with change? Are constant innovations at your place of employment forcing you to spend time continually learning and comprehending new information or learning to use new technological equipment? Do you wish you had the comprehension power to learn the information required at your job more rapidly?

Do you wish you could better comprehend what you study and read? Are you frustrated by having to spend more time rereading because you cannot comprehend what you read or learned the first time? Do you feel so hopeless that you do not think you can comprehend much at all?

Take heart! You can successfully improve your reading comprehension quickly to learn anything you want. This book can help anyone of any age, whether you are:

- a senior citizen or baby-boomer who want to increase your reading comprehension and keep it sharp
- a job seeker who want to comprehend information for a job or career
- a teacher who wants teaching methods, techniques, and strategies to help your students improve reading comprehension for better grades or test scores
- a parent who want to improve your child or teen's grades
- a student who wants to improve your reading comprehension, study skills, note taking, or test-taking skills for the ACT or SAT, state reading tests, high school placement test, or college boards
- a parent who wants to know how to raise a gifted and talented child with strong reading comprehension skills from the time he or she is a baby or toddler
- a trainer or employer who wants to be more effective in helping trainees or employees comprehend their new job skills
- a sports coach who wants your football, basketball, baseball, soccer, golf, gymnastics, or hockey players to learn and comprehend the sports play book faster and better and help your athletes improve -a person who wants to learn how to comprehend new vocabulary words in Spanish, French, German, or any language for school, a job or a career
- a person of any age who needs to learn and comprehend English vocabulary words
- an adult who wants to improve relationships and communication skills by knowing how others comprehend

- a supervisor, employer, employee, co-worker, or customer who wants to communicate better with others on the job by knowing how they comprehend best
- a doctor, psychiatrist, psychologist or social worker who wants to help clients and patients improve their comprehension
- anyone who has a hobby, skill, or passion you want to pursue and learn and comprehend quickly.

This book gives you fast, easy strategies to help you improve your reading comprehension quickly.

Advances in science, particularly neuroscience, have helped us better understand the way our brain works. Although this knowledge has been in laboratories, research centers, and scientific journals for years, few people have applied it to make our everyday life easier.

Some of these advances have gradually become public knowledge over the past few decades. Unfortunately, many educational institutions throughout the world are still in the dark ages when it comes to these advanced brain-based learning techniques. This book gives every person a method to learn and comprehend successfully and quickly. It is user-friendly and simple to follow. It is written for everyone: for people of all ages, at all levels of education, and is designed to help every person improve reading comprehension quickly.

You will learn strategies and techniques to rapidly improve your reading comprehension that can be applied to any field you choose. Once you have improved your reading comprehension you will be able to use these methods for the rest of your life for anything you wish to learn. This book will help you find the path to increasing your reading comprehension in a way that works best for you.

Follow the fast, easy, and simple steps in the book and you will emerge from the last page of this book an expert on how *you* comprehend best and how to apply it to any field you want.

What Is a Reading Comprehension Learning Style, Brain Hemispheric Preference or Your Best Reading Comprehension Superlink?

We each have a different way of learning and comprehending. Each of us has a reading comprehension **superlink** that makes comprehending anything faster, easier, and more comfortable. Your reading comprehension superlink is the easiest method for you to improve your comprehension of information in order to understand it, remember it, and retain it; it links to our brain information we want to comprehend in a super-fast way. Your reading comprehension superlink is a combination of your best learning style and the part of the brain you use to process and store information. Each of us learns and comprehends differently. Some comprehend best what they read, whereas others comprehend best what they hear. Your reading comprehension learning style is the way you receive information from the world.

What are the four main reading comprehension learning styles? The main ways of learning and comprehending are visual, auditory, tactile, and kinesthetic, or a combination of these. **Visual learners** comprehend best through seeing, either printed or graphic material, or their surroundings. **Auditory learners** comprehend best by hearing, listening, and talking.

10

Tactile learners comprehend best through tactile sensation and by touching objects, experiencing information through their feelings, or using their hands and fingers. **Kinesthetic learners** comprehend best by doing action and moving their large motor muscles.

Some people use two, three, or all four learning style modalities to comprehend.

After we use our reading comprehension learning style to comprehend information, our brain processes and stores the information either using the left side (left hemisphere) of the brain or the right side (right hemisphere) or a combination of the two. Each side has a different comprehension style, or its own way of thinking about and looking at the world. Some of us have a **left- brain hemispheric preference** and some have a **right- brain hemispheric preference**, while some use both sides of the brain. **Left-brain learners** tend to be sequential and comprehend information in a linear manner. **Right-brain learners** tend to comprehend globally, seeing the big picture, and connecting seemingly unrelated ideas. Also, left-brain learners comprehend better in symbols such as letters, words, and numbers, while right-brain learners comprehend better using sensory images of sights, sounds, smell, tastes, and touch, and movement, without words.

By determining *your* reading comprehension learning style and *your* brain hemispheric preference, you can find your reading comprehension superlink— your fastest style of comprehending. There are eight superlinks reading comprehension learning styles and brain styles to improve reading comprehension: **visual left-brain, visual right-brain, auditory left-brain, auditory right-brain, tactile left-brain, tactile right- brain, kinesthetic left-brain,** and **kinesthetic right- brain.**

When someone is instructing us in a different way than the one that matches our best style, it is uncomfortable, unnatural, and stressful, and we do not learn and comprehend as effectively and quickly. For example, think about the hand you use for writing. You have become so used to using that hand that it has become automatic; you do not even think about it.

However, if you were asked to write with the opposite hand, it may be difficult, awkward, slower, and uncomfortable. You could *force* yourself to use that hand, but it would be a struggle. You would be so busy concentrating on getting your hand to write that you may not even be able to focus on what it is you are supposed to be writing. It is the same with our reading comprehension learning style. When we learn through our reading comprehension superlink, comprehending is fast, easy, effortless, and automatic. When we comprehend through a learning link that is not easy for us, comprehending becomes a struggle.

How You Can Benefit from Knowing Your Best Reading Comprehension Superlink Learning Style and Brain Style: Improving Your Reading Comprehension to Learn Quickly, Improve Your Study and Test-Taking Skills, and Increase Test Scores

By discovering your best superlink reading comprehension learning style and brain style, you will know how to improve reading comprehension, gain the ability to learn quickly, have strategies to study better, and increase your test scores. You will comprehend reading material better, making your study time more productive. Those who have used these techniques have drastically improved their scores on tests—whether for school tests, state or high-stakes reading tests, entrance examinations such as the ACT, SAT, High School Placement Test, college boards, certification exams, or qualifying tests for a job or career.

Improving Your Communication and Relationships Issues and Problems with Others

Not only can you comprehend faster, you will learn how others' superlinks reading comprehension learning styles work, making you a better communicator, trainer, and instructor when you work with, train, or teach others. Do you have relationship issues and problems with others and want relationship advice? You can improve communication with those with whom you live or with whom you are in a relationship. Have you ever been frustrated because you spent an hour trying to give your child homework help and he or she still did not comprehend it? Knowledge of the eight reading comprehension superlinks gets your message across effectively. Whether you work in an office, a corporation, a factory, a store, or anywhere else, by identifying others' reading comprehension learning links you will be able to communicate more effectively with your boss, co-workers, employees, and customers, and improve relationships with them. You will find a new power to get your message across in a way that others can understand.

It has helped instructors train others in academic and nonacademic subjects such as learning a job, an art, a hobby, or a sport. For example, instructors who worked at the

Michael Jordan Golf Company, Director of Instruction and 1993 PGA Teacher of the Year, Charlie Long, and Golf Instructor and Missouri State Amateur Gold Champion, Maria Long, have said, We have utilized learning styles while giving golf instruction for several years now. As teachers, it was a major source of frustration to give out what we knew was good information, only to see widely varied results with our learners. What we originally passed off as greater or lesser degrees of talent in our students we now recognize was due to the fact that we did not always give the information in our students' best way of receiving it. We now adapt our approach to the learners—a gold lesson can be a lengthy video viewing session; a richly detailed conversation; a hands-on walk through a new motion; or just a super-visual coaching session with short do instructions. We have greater peace of mind, and our students obviously love their progress. We feel that adapting to the student's learning style is maybe the real future of golf instruction. We know more than enough ways to swing—we just need better ways to help others understand. Their appreciation to the future of golf instruction holds equally true for instruction in all fields.

Small differences in communication due to various reading comprehension learning styles can stress even the closest relationship. Understanding how you and other individuals learn and comprehend best can also greatly improve your personal relationships and communication with the significant others in your life.

This book, *How to Improve Reading Comprehension Quickly by Knowing Your Personal Reading Comprehension Style: Quick, Easy Tips to Improve Comprehension through the Brain's Fastest Superlinks Learning Style*, is like eight books in one—a book for each of the eight superlinks reading comprehension styles and brain styles. You can read the whole book cover to cover, in order, or read only those sections that relate to your own reading comprehension superlink, skipping the descriptions and strategies that do not relate to you. After you understand how to improve reading comprehension through your own reading comprehension superlink you may want to go back and read through the book again to learn about how people with other superlinks comprehend.

Note: If you do not know you or your family's and friend's superlink reading comprehension style and brain style, you can either read through the descriptions in this book to see which reading comprehension style(s) describe you, or you may wish to take a learning style inventory test or take the Superlinks to Accelerated Learning™ learning style and brain style inventory test before, while, or after reading the book. You can find instructions in the special Bonus for Readers section in the back of this book, *How to Improve Reading Comprehension Quickly by Knowing Your Personal Reading Comprehension Style*, on how to get to the website to take the online learning style inventory test which is instantly scored with your personalized report.

Have fun mastering techniques to improve reading comprehension rapidly!

CHAPTER 2:

FIND YOUR FASTEST WAY TO IMPROVE YOUR READING COMPREHENSION QUICKLY USING REVOLUTIONARY BRAIN-BASED STRATEGIES

You *can* learn how to comprehend any subject quickly. You can increase your reading comprehension of whatever you read or learn by knowing your brain's fastest way of comprehending. Whether you need to comprehend material for study skills, note taking, or test- taking skills for a test, or learn and comprehend new skills on the job, these revolutionary techniques can improve your comprehension.

Many people worry that their current ability to comprehend is fixed and cannot be improved. Others worry about comprehension loss as one ages. However, take heart! Medical breakthroughs have revealed the brain's power of plasticity. Molded by experiences in the past, the brain is also capable of establishing new pathways for learning and comprehending. This exciting revolutionary discovery about brain plasticity means that we can change the way we comprehend, think, and learn. We are no longer restricted to limitations that have formed us so far; we can shape our future.

For over thirty-five years I have witnessed the astounding successes people have enjoyed using these revolutionary brain-based reading comprehension strategies I developed and applied based on research on how the brain learns and comprehends. I am excited to share with readers in this book these easy-to-use techniques for comprehending anything quickly. One of the approaches I developed, Virtual Reality Reading™, as part of the Superlinks to Accelerated Learning™ and Keys to Reading Success™ reading comprehension program, is based on research that when people inwardly experience in their brain what they are reading, using their fastest way of learning, their brain comprehends it as well as if it were actually experienced outwardly. Our brain not only comprehends better, but new, more effective patterns of learning and reading comprehension are set up in the brain to ensure mastery of any subject. The brain's ability to form new neural pathways, based on these accelerated learning and reading comprehension techniques, can alter and improve one's mental performance and retention.

An exciting breakthrough scientifically confirms the mechanism by which the Virtual Reality Reading comprehension and memory technique has worked.

Science has advanced so that the mechanism by which the brain learns can be demonstrated through medical scanning techniques. With the development of more precise scanning equipment such PET scans (positive emission tomography), Functional MRI's (functional Magnetic Resonance Imaging), and TMS (transcranial magnetic stimulation) used in experimental studies, evidence has surfaced that shows that by thinking about a task, new pathways in the brain develop as if someone had actually physically performed the task.

For example, Alvaro Pascual-Leone, a neuroscientist at Harvard Medical School, performed an experiment in which one group of people practiced a piano exercise using five fingers for two hours a day for five days. Each day, they took a TMS test in which a coil of wire held above their head sent a short magnetic pulse into the motor cortex of their brain. This allowed the scientist to observe the activity of neurons or nerve cells in that part of the brain. The TMS test helped the researchers map how much of the motor cortex controlled the finger movements to play the piano. After observing the results for five days, the scientists discovered that the part of the motor cortex used for these finger exercises on the piano spread to surrounding areas of the motor cortex. This revealed that extended connections were being made as the participants continued to practice the piano. That result was expected. Practicing playing the piano stimulated neurons that increased connections in the brain and expanded the amount of brain space devoted to that task. What was fascinating to the scientists though, and which bears out the Virtual Reality Reading™ comprehension and memory improvement technique, was what happened to the second group of people involved in the experiment.

The second group was asked to only *think* about playing the same five-finger piano exercise for two hours a day, for five days a week, without actually playing the piano. Neuron activity in the motor cortex also was measured by the TMS test. The scientists then compared the group that played the piano and the group that only imagined themselves playing the piano. The astounding results revealed that the group that imagined themselves playing the piano showed the same expansion of neuron activity in the region of the motor cortex as did those who actually played the instrument. Pascual-Leone later wrote, Mental practice resulted in a similar reorganization of the brain (from How the Brain Rewires Itself, *Time Magazine*, Jan. 19, 2007, by Sharon Begley). This experiment shows the power of mental training to change brain connections. This news is exciting because the general principles that I had discovered about learning and comprehension through research and application over thirty years was being proven through advanced instrumentation such as the TMS test.

This revolutionary Virtual Reality Reading™ comprehension and memory improvement technique forms one part of accelerated learning. The power of thought can form neural connections in the brain as if one physically performed a task. We know that most people can tell you what they did this morning or what they did yesterday. They can comprehend events in which they physically participated. The Virtual Reality Reading™ comprehension and memory improvement strategies translate what is read into visualization of the material as if one were participating so that one can establish brain connections as if one had done the activity. The enhanced brain connections that are formed can more easily be stored and retrieved as memories and thus help the learner comprehend more information.

The next discovery supporting the Virtual Reality Reading™ comprehension and memory improvement program is that we all do not comprehend in the same way. People of all ages, all genders, all walks of life, all cultures, and all nationalities have taken the two learning style inventory and brain style tests I developed: Superlinks to Accelerated Learning™ test, which contains the Linksman Learning Style Preference Assessment™ test and the Linksman Brain Hemispheric Preference Assessment™ test. The results reveal that people comprehend, remember, and learn in different ways. Their fastest way of learning and comprehending is connected to how they take in and comprehend information from the world around them into their brain. Through a combination of nature and nurture, (genetics mingled with stimulation from the senses to the brain through life experiences), our brain takes in information differently. These experiences have established neural networks that are familiar, comfortable, and automatic in each of us. When we learn and comprehend through that pathway, we learn faster and more effectively and retain the information. Thus, when we know what our fastest pathway is and use techniques that are based on those pathways, we can learn faster and comprehend better.

By finding your fastest way of learning how to comprehend, you can increase reading comprehension, recall, and memory of any subject. People of all ages have found a dramatic difference in their ability to comprehend when they used their fastest reading comprehension superlink.

It is important to receive the right diagnosis of your best way of comprehending. For the past thirty years I have researched, developed, and field-tested what many educators consider to be the most accurate and comprehensive learning reading comprehension style and brain style assessment inventory test for determining one's fastest way of learning and comprehending. To date, when anyone has taken this learning preference assessment and altered their learning and reading comprehension techniques to their fastest way of comprehending, they experienced a significant improvement in their ability to learn and comprehend.

This has been more than anecdotal reporting. For example, I have applied this Superlinks to Accelerated Learning methodology to my learn-to-read program called Keys to Reading Success™. Through studies using the Keys to Reading Success™ reading comprehension and memory improvement program (which includes reading tests, reading practice, and memory strategies for kindergarten, grades one to twelve, college, and adult learners) measurements of reading test scores and reading performance in public schools (from elementary, middle, and high schools) revealed that from 88% to 99% of all students rose an average of two, three, four, and five years of growth in reading within months. This includes students who were in Regular Education programs as well as students in Special Education, Title I, Remedial Reading, At-risk, Gifted, and ELL (English language learners), ESL or ESOL (English as a Second Language), and Bi-lingual programs or those challenged by ADHD (Attention deficit hyperactivity disorder) or ADD (attention-deficit disorder). The other 1% or 2%, comprised mostly those in the categories of severe or profound mental retardation, who did not make gains of two or more grade levels in a few months, but did make gains of several months, which exceeded their previous performance without using their superlinks reading comprehension learning style. Since reading forms the basis of learning for a majority of subjects, improving and accelerating reading progress can make a significant difference in learning those subjects. The Keys to Reading Success™ reading comprehension and memory strategies helps learners of all ages become top readers, able to comprehend and remember what one read for assignments in a course, a job, or a reading test in any content area subject. They are able to retain in long-term memory what one reads for mastery in any field. Thus, anyone who needs to learn a subject that requires comprehending what one reads can dramatically improve his or her ability in that subject.

Thirty-five years of success stories document how people

of all ages have experienced a dramatic improvement in learning and reading comprehension based on the revolutionary techniques in this book. Superlinks brain-based reading comprehension strategies have helped people of all ages be successful. Here are a few case studies to illustrate the wide range of people it has helped:

Case Study 1: From Two Years of Not Reading a Single Word to Learning to Read in a Day

A first-grade boy from Virginia who had been left back in kindergarten for two years and was labeled as ADHD could not read a single word despite numerous attempts at school to teach him even first grade reading skills. His grandfather, a retired Navy pilot, observing the boy was bright, was puzzled as to why he could not learn to read. When his grandfather did some research on the Internet and discovered our revolutionary reading program based on accelerated reading comprehension and memory learning techniques, Keys to Reading Success™, he flew his grandson from Virginia to Naperville, Illinois, in the western suburbs of the Chicago area, to see if he could be helped. The Keys to Reading Success™ reading diagnostic test was given along with the Superlinks to Accelerated Learning™ learning style inventory tests. The reading diagnostic test confirmed that the boy could not read a single first-grade reading level word and was, in fact, at a kindergarten level in reading, although he was the age of a second- grade student. The superlinks learning style and brain style inventory tests showed that he was a kinesthetic right-brain learner who remembered best what he did kines-thetically. After the boy spent only two hours in a reading session using a kinesthetic right-brain learning reading comprehension, phonics, and memory technique, he was able to read a list of first grade words and the first pages of a book fluently by himself for the first time in his life and comprehend it. The boy was beaming, and the grandfather shed tears of joy. They continued the technique for a period of two weeks and the boy was able to read an entire sixty-page book consisting of full-page stories at a first-grade reading level. Excited at finally being able to read, the boy clutched the book to his chest with pride, asking whoever passed him by whether they wanted to listen to him read aloud! Within months he was reading at a first-grade reading level and had renewed confidence and self-esteem that he was not stupid after all. He was taken off ADHD medication as it was medically confirmed that his reading problem was not due to having an attention-deficit hyperactive disorder but was merely a result of his being a kinesthetic right-brain learner who only needed the correct techniques for his unique way of learning and remembering to teach him how to learn to read.

Case Study 2: Never Too Old to Learn to Read

A baby-boomer gentleman in his fifties, who spent his whole life believing he could not read, decided that he wanted to give it once last chance—he wanted to be able to learn to read a book. When his Superlink memory learning and brain style, or fastest way of learning and remembering, was discovered, and the correct reading comprehension and memory techniques were used, he was also able to read successfully, opening new doorways for his life. He later said, I wish I had discovered this reading comprehension and memory technique as a child, as it would have dramatically changed the course of my life.

Case Study 3: The School District that No One Thought Could Raise Reading Test Scores

An entire school district in an area of low economic income, southwest of Chicago, near Joliet, Illinois, had been not meeting state standards in their state reading tests for six consecutive years and was on the state warning list, or probation. Lack of academic success had spiraled into a school with severe discipline problems, lack of motivation, and a cynicism towards any new reading program ever working since none had worked so far. Students in the entire school district went through a Keys to Reading Success™ reading diagnostic test and a superlinks test of learning styles and brain hemispheric preference. Accelerated learning and memory techniques in reading (reading comprehension, memory improvement, phonics, fluency, vocabulary, note taking, study skills, and test-taking skills for the Illinois ISAT state reading tests) were used with the students to match each of their fastest way of learning.

Within six months, the students raised their reading levels on average growth of two to five years above their grade level, and for the first time they met state standards in reading on their state reading test. Discipline problems dropped to the point where the in-school suspension officer, who was used to numerous discipline referrals a day, said, Now I am lonely as I hardly get any discipline referrals in my office. Students are engaged and excited about learning for the first time, and their discipline has improved.

Case Study 4: A School with 83% Non-English Speaking Students that Rose to Third Highest Reading Scores in the District in One Year

An elementary school in which 83% of the student population spoke Spanish as their primary language and were learning English as a second language had not yet met state reading standards as tested on the Illinois ISAT reading test. By finding each student's superlink learning style and brain style, or fastest way of learning, and then using the Keys to Reading Success™ reading comprehension and memory program to teach them to read fluently and remember vocabulary in English, including all the phonics and decoding patterns, in their unique learning memory and brain styles, they met state standards in reading and came in third highest in the East Aurora school district.

Case Study 5: From Failure to Success in One Year in an East Los Angeles, California, Charter School

A charter school in East Los Angeles, California, was opened to focus on Afro-American culture (CLAS, an acronym for the Culture and Language Academy of Success) as it attempted to raise student reading achievement. The parents, wanting to see improved educational opportunities for their children, received permission from the Los Angeles Unified School District to form a charter school. At first, the students had not met state reading standards, but after adopting the revolutionary accelerated learning and memory techniques in the Keys to Reading Success™ reading comprehension and memory improvement program and its Superlinks to

Accelerated Learning™ learning and memory style and brain style inventory tests, the charter school met the California state reading standards within one school year. Using the brain-based methods of accelerated learning and memory based on Superlinks™ and Keys to Reading Success™, their dedicated teaching staff was trained in these methods, and within less than one school year, the elementary school improved their reading test scores and showed the highest growth in reading scores in the entire Los Angeles Unified School District.

Case Study 6: ACT Reading Test Scores Improved Dramatically in Months

Students who had scored in the low teens on their reading ACT test (college entrance exams) improved their reading test scores to the high twenties and into the thirties in a matter of months using reading comprehension, memory, study skills, and test-taking techniques that matched their fastest way of learning and remembering, enabling them to score high enough to be accepted into college.

Case Study 7: Raising Preschoolers and Kindergarteners Reading Levels to Become Top First Grade Readers and Place in Advanced, Gifted, and Enriched Programs

In a school in a high minority and high poverty area, reading scores had been so low that the community, the parents, and even the teachers believed it hopeless that any of the students could ever learn. However, using accelerated reading comprehension, phonics, fluency, and memory techniques

27

that matched their superlinks memory and learning and brain styles, preschoolers and kindergarteners were able to learn how to read at a first- and second- grade reading level within less than a year so that when they entered first grade, they were at the top of their class in reading. This progress continued and as they entered second grade and third grade and higher, many ended up qualifying for advanced, gifted and talented, and enrichment programs. Their reading levels improved to between two and eight years *above* their age. In fact, ten of them who were previously thought to be unable to learn were placed into a gifted program at a gifted and talented magnet school. When the teachers realized how these new reading and memory techniques they were trained to use had produced such startling results by the end of the school year, some had tears come to their eyes to see that their students were not dumb or stupid after all but just needed the key to their brains and learning how to learn in their best way of learning and remembering. Many teachers felt renewed passion for teaching when they saw that it was not hopeless and they could make a difference in the lives of their students once they knew how.

Case Study 8: A Losing University Football Team Has Its First Winning Season through Superlinks Reading Comprehension and Memory Strategies

A university football team that never had a winning season tested all the athletes for their superlink learning and brain styles. The athletic coaches were trained in using each player's superlink memory, learning, and brain styles to teach the football playbook. After altering the football coaches' teaching styles to match each of the player's superlink memory and learning style, the football team had their first winning season! Applying these techniques to academic subjects, they were also able to improve reading test scores to do better in their content subject area classes.

Case Study 9: College Students, Medical School Students, Professionals in all Fields, and Athletes Helped through Brain-based Accelerated Reading Comprehension and Learning Methods

Medical students have been able to raise their scores on their medical examinations using these revolutionary methods. Professionals in all fields, including business, law, finances, technology, medicine, and real estate, have been able to improve their on-the- job performance and improve on certification examinations using the Superlink accelerated learning, reading comprehension, and memory techniques.

Athletes and coaches have used these reading comprehension techniques to improve sports performance in areas such as football and golf.

Write Your Own Success Story

Techniques in this book can also help you identify your fastest way of comprehending and learning so you can write your own success story. Once you know your own brain's secrets, you too can use it to improve reading comprehension to learn anything quickly.

Readers are invited to share your success stories by sending them in if you want to share them to give hope to others who may be frustrated or struggling with reading comprehension as you once did!

CHAPTER 3:

DIFFERENCES IN HOW PEOPLE WITH DIFFERENT LEARNING STYLES COMPREHEND INFORMATION FROM THE WORLD AROUND THEM

Why do we have a preference for one mode of comprehending over another? It is all about the technology of the brain. What form of stimulation did we receive more of as we were growing up? Did our caretakers give us many objects, pictures, mobiles, or illustrated books at which to look? Was there much talking, conversation, dialogue, or music in our childhood? Maybe we were given a great amount of hands-on activities to do like finger-painting, stringing beads, coloring, board games, or toys that required the use of our hands and fingers. Were we encouraged to be more actively engaged in running, jumping, crawling, swimming, playing ball, building with blocks, making play-houses, or doing competitive activities? Whatever stimulation we received, our brains were grooving reading comprehension pathways along those lines. Over time, those networks of sensory pathways became more firmly established and more automatic. When something is automatic we do not have to think about it—it comes easily. Thus, we feel more comfortable and learn how to comprehend faster when working through that modality.

Over thirty years of interviewing and assessing the reading comprehension and learning style and brain style preferences of people from all walks of life, there are certain patterns of behavior, thought, comprehension, and memory that identify those who have one sensory preference over another. Let us take the scenario of a person entering a room. The experience is different for people who have a different reading comprehension and learning style preference. The information that comes in, how the person comprehends the experience, and how he or she remembers it is different for people of various learning and reading comprehension styles. Of course, there are people who learn through a combination of two or more learning and reading comprehension styles and some who use all of them! Depending upon the preference, or the combination, that room provides a different experience for each of them.

How a Visual Learner Comprehends Input from the World

If a growing child has received more stimulation through the pathways involving seeing, then that person relies more on that sense when taking in, comprehending, and remembering stimulation from the world. When this person enters a room, what is most noticed and comprehended are the visuals—the color of the room, the paintings hanging on the walls, the size and shape of the furniture, printed material such as magazines or newspapers, and what people look like. They may notice or recall anything that is out of order or not matching color-wise. They are attuned visually to the room. When they think about, comprehend, and remember their experience, they focus on what they were seeing. When they have to remember the room, they remember best what they saw. Over time, they identify themselves as a visual learner who comprehends visually.

How an Auditory Learner Comprehends Input from the World

If a child grows up exposed to a lot of conversation and dialogue or music and sounds, then the pathways for comprehending auditory input are more developed. Thus, when this person enters a room, the auditory stimulus is most noticed and recalled. This person will notice and remember the sounds in the room, such as talking, dialogue, conversation, the noise of passing cars, the whirl of a fan or hum of a computer, or a cell phone ringing in another room. This person will notice and recall best what people are saying and the sound of their voices. Thus, when they think about, comprehend, or remember their experience in the room, they focus on what sounds they were hearing or what people were saying. When they have to remember the room, they remember best what they heard. Thus, they develop a preference for being an auditory learner who comprehends best auditorially.

How a Tactile Learner Comprehends Input from the World

If a child has been exposed to activity involving using the hands or fingers, or there is a lot of stimulus on the skin, such as variations in heat and cold, softness and hardness, roughness and smoothness, pleasant or unpleasant sensations, or a lot of intensity of feelings either verbally expressed or nonverbally communicated, then the tactile modality for comprehension has received more stimulation in the brain's neural pathways. When such a person enters a room, he or she notices and recalls the nonverbal communication as expressed through people's body language, facial expressions, or tones of voice, plus the feelings they get from others or from the room itself. This person will focus on and comprehend what can be touched or felt, or what the hands can do in the room, such as feeling a soft couch, writing, picking up objects to hold, and any other hands- on activity. This person will focus on hands-on experiences or the feelings they got from the room or from people. When remembering the experience, this person will remember best what was felt and what was touched using the hands. Therefore, they develop a preference for being a tactile learner or comprehending tactilely.

How a Kinesthetic Learner Comprehends Input from the World

If a child has had much stimulation through movement of his or her body and large muscles, then that pathway becomes more comfortable for that learner.

When this person enters a room, the first question that arises is, What can I do here? This person looks for space to move around, physical activities that can be done, and some challenge by which a goal can be achieved or won. When processing and remembering the experience, this person focuses on the action in the room. When trying to remember the room, this person best remembers what he or she did in the room. They then develop a preference for being a kinesthetic learner, comprehending kinesthetically.

Learning and Reading Comprehension Style Alone is Only Part of the Process

Besides comprehending through our fastest learning and reading comprehension style, the information is further processed in the brain. Some people process and comprehend things in a sequential or step-by-step order. Others process and comprehend information by getting the big picture or main idea first and then fitting in the details. Medical researchers have previously identified that sequential thinking processes take place in the left side of the brain, and the global overview thinking processes happen in the right side of the brain. Whether one subscribes to that distinction or not, or as brain research identifies exactly where they take place, for the purposes of defining the two types of processing and comprehending, sequential thinking is referred to in this book as left brain, while global thinking is referred to as right brain. Whether science later proves sequential thought is somewhere else does not matter so much as knowing that we want to learn and comprehend new things sequentially as opposed to learning and comprehending new things through a global overview that does not focus on steps in order. The reading comprehension technique that matches how we learn and comprehend is what matters most when we are learning and comprehending, no matter what terms are used for them, or where they are actually taking place in the brain.

Similarly, besides the order in which we process and comprehend information, we also process and comprehend through words or images. Some people think and comprehend more in words. They talk to themselves and think about what is happening through language. Some

35

people think and comprehend more in terms of pictures. They recall images, colors, shapes, designs, faces, and patterns and comprehend these the best. Some comprehend equally through both. Again, whether words vs. graphics or pictures are actually localized in one part of the brain is not as important as knowing that is how we comprehend information faster. For the sake and ease of terminology, in this book, in recognition that brain science is identifying multiple areas of the brain in which various processes take place, comprehending through words will be referred to as left-brain functioning; and comprehending through images or pictures will be referred to as right-brain functioning. Knowing whether we need text or pictures when we comprehend can help us accelerate our comprehension, memory, and mastery of a subject, irrespective of the parts of the brain in each individual case such functions are actually taking place.

Your Superlink is the Combination of Your Reading Comprehension Learning Style and Brain Hemispheric Preference

In the early 1970s, work was done regarding learning styles. In those days, people were classified as one of three styles: visual, auditory, and kinesthetic.

Later, the term tactile was lumped in with kinesthetic, keeping the classification as three styles. In over thirty years of work, I was one of the few who recognized that a tactile learner is extremely different from a kinesthetic learner. Tactile and kinesthetic learners are two distinct types of learners and have different learning needs. Thus, I separate learning styles into four categories. In the early 1980s, as I used learning style teaching methods and reading comprehension techniques to teach people, I also observed repeatedly that visual learners were not all the same. I realize that some visual learners focused on printed words in text, while others focused on pictures, images, and graphics.

This same phenomena occurred with auditory learners. Some auditory learners were great at comprehending lectures, while other auditory learners could not repeat a word of a lecture in a university hall if their life depended on it. Yet, they may have been highly aware of sounds, music, and sound effects.

I also realized that not all tactile learners were alike. Some focused on writing words, while others were not good at writing but excelled in drawing or making hands-on projects. Some were able to express their feelings in words, while others expressed their feelings through nonverbal communication.

Finally, not all kinesthetic people were alike.

Some liked to learn by verbal instructions, and others got annoyed when anyone spoke when they were engaged in activity. They preferred instead nonverbal demonstration that they could copy. Some kinesthetic people liked to talk about what they did, while others did not want to talk at all about the physical experiences in which they engaged.

Through these observations, I discovered that some visual learners were left-brain thinkers, while other visual learners were right-brain thinkers. There were visual left-brain learners who learned faster and comprehended better by seeing text; and there were visual right brain learners who learned faster and comprehended better by seeing pictures or graphics. The same was true of the other learning and comprehension styles. I saw dramatic increases in learning speed and reading comprehension when the learning style and brain hemispheric preference comprehension techniques were combined. I thus coined the term superlink to describe the combination of one's learning style and brain hemispheric preference to comprehend best. I thus named the strategies as the Superlinks to Accelerated Learning™. Since the 1980s, I have tracked the use of superlinks in the teaching of reading with entire bodies of students in schools, from elementary school, to middle school and high school, and to college students, and adults in various professions. Without fail, people were able to learn faster, comprehend better, and master any subject when taught in their superlink style—the combination of learning and reading comprehension style and brain hemispheric preference style.

This accelerated system of reading comprehension was so effective, I created an entire pre- K, kindergarten, grade one through grade twelve, and college and adult reading curriculum program based on this Superlinks to Accelerated Learning™ and named it Keys to Reading Success™. This method has been studied and researched and have proven time and again to raise reading levels of 88%-99% of all students in a school anywhere from two, three, four, or five grade reading levels—on average—within months. The longest time for these gains to take place has been six to eight months, and has occurred as rapidly as two to four months' time. This includes students who are in Regular Education, Gifted, Special Education, Title I, or Remedial Reading programs, students with ADHD and ADD, and students who need to learn English who are in ELL (English language learners), ESL or ESOL (English as a Second Language), or Bilingual or Dual Language programs. It works to improve reading levels in both males and females. It works for people of all cultures or language groups. It works for people of all ages, from the very young to adults who have retired. Using the Superlinks to Accelerated Learning™ technique with the Keys to Reading Success™ reading comprehension and memory improvement program has helped students become top readers, to comprehend what they read, to remember what was read for an assignment or test, and to retain in long-term memory what was read for mastery in any field.

For this reason, it is recommended that one take both the Superlinks Learning Style Preference Assessment™ tests and the Brain Hemispheric Preference Assessment™ inventory tests for the most complete and comprehension diagnosis of one's best and fastest way of learning and comprehending.

Knowing Your Learning and Reading Comprehension Style Can Speed Up Your Learning

As our brain takes in the world through the filter of our learning style, or combination of styles, that network of thinking is easier to use for comprehending, learning, and remembering. In our unique learning and reading comprehension style, we take in information faster, focus on comprehending and thinking about what we learned, and recall and memorize the material better. These variations in strategies can help us learn how to learn and comprehend any subject faster. If we know our own unique way of learning and comprehending, we can use that information to help us comprehend any subject more rapidly. It will open doors for us to comprehend more and learn more quickly. Knowing the keys to our own brain's comprehension can help us ask for what we need from an instructor, and if not provided by that teacher, help us provide for ourselves the strategy to master any subject. If the learning environment in which we find ourselves does not match the way we comprehend faster, we will have some strategies to use by ourselves to translate any subject into the way we need to recall it so we are independent and can learn and comprehend, even on our own.

I developed the Virtual Reality Reading™ comprehension and memory improvement strategies to help you take in information that you read in your best and fastest way of comprehending. Once you know this technique, it forms the basis of many other comprehension tasks, study skills, memory skills, and test-taking skills. You can use this virtual reality reading comprehension and memory technique to effectively learn and comprehend anything quickly.

Beyond this technique, there are many other skills and teaching methods needed to master any subject. Building on the virtual reality comprehension and memory techniques is a series of skills. These are all designed to increase comprehension and memory of whatever one is learning.

PART 2:
FIND YOUR SUPERLINK TO
COMPREHENDING ANYTHING QUICKLY

CHAPTER 4:
FIND YOUR SUPERLINKS
COMPREHENSION STYLE PREFERENCE
AND BRAIN HEMISPHERIC PREFERENCE

How to Take the Superlinks Linksman Learning Style Preference Assessment™ and Linksman Brain Hemispheric Preference Assessment™ Inventory Tests

Over the years, thousands of people have requested that I score the test for them, to ensure accuracy and save them time. To save even further time and make it easy for people, I spent five years converting it into an online assessment test that people could easily take using the computer, so the program could be instantly scored and provide detailed complete and instant results. The online test is now available in three places: www.readinginstruction.com or through www.superlinkslearning.com, or through the accelerated reading program for grades pre-K, Kindergarten, Grade One through Grade Twelve, college, and adult reading, called Keys to Reading Success, at www.keystoreadingsuccess.com. The test is the same whether taken in any of these three websites. One is associated with Keys to Reading Success™, pre-K, kindergarten, and Grade 1 through Grade 12, college, and adult reading program to teach both how to learn to read and how to improve in memory and reading, including reading and listening comprehension, memory, phonics, fluency, vocabulary, phonemic awareness, study skills, note taking, and test-taking skills in reading and in any content area subject. Once you take the online learning style and brain style inventory tests, you will get your instantly-scored personalized results with a detailed report on how you comprehend the best, what materials you need, what is the best learning environment, what are the best learning and comprehension tips and strategies, and how you best communicate with others and want others to communicate with you.

When you take the Superlinks online assessment tests to determine your learning and reading comprehension style and brain style, it is highly recommended that you answer the questions as accurately as possible. If you do not answer these accurately, the results may indicate that you have a different learning and reading comprehension style or brain hemispheric preference than what you really prefer, and you will not be learning and comprehending in your most effective way. For each superlinks learning and reading comprehension style and brain style, there are different methods to use, and it would be ineffective for you to use the wrong technique. So, be as accurate as you can—as painful as it may be for some!

The key to answering the questions is to select the answers or choices that are most natural or comfortable for you. Although we may be able to make ourselves behave in ways described in the other choices—and we often have to do that on the job or in other situations—one choice will probably feel best for us if left to our own devices. Just as we can force ourselves to write with our non-dominant hand, we may also force ourselves to behave in two, three, or four different ways (described in each question) depending on the circumstance. The question to ask yourself is, Which way feels the best and is the least stressful? It is in that spirit that you should respond to the questions.

What happens if you truly feel you can select more than one choice? It may be that for some of the questions, you absolutely know that two or three choices (and some people, even all the choices) are equally true of you. In that case, go ahead and select all those that equally describe you. First try to settle on one choice, and if you are sure that there is more than one best answer, then select the others also.

When you have completed taking the *Linksman Learning Style Preference Assessment*™ test, next take the *Brain Hemispheric Preference Assessment*™ test to find out your preference for which of the functions of the two hemispheres of the brain you use for understanding the stimulus you receive from the world and for comprehending and storing the information. Just as you did in the learning style preference assessment, you will be selecting the best of two choices that is most natural, comfortable, and stress-free for you.

If you absolutely feel that both answers are really you, then select both answers. That too is a brain hemispheric preference style. Make sure you do not choose both to take the easy way out and to rush through the assessment test. If you have to choose both answers, do it because you have given it full consideration and know for certain that both describe you equally well.

After taking the *Learning Style Preference Assessment*™ and the *Brain Hemispheric Preference Assessment*™ tests the results are automatically scored to find your best reading comprehension superlink.

Since the 1980s, when I began using learning and reading

comprehension styles and brain hemispheric preferences, I realized there was a difference between those who were visual learners with a right-brain preference and those who were visuals with a left-brain preference. Similarly, there were auditory learners with a right-brain preference and some with a left-brain preference, and the way these two groups learned and comprehended differed vastly. While teachers who used learning styles would only assess whether their students were visual, auditory, tactile, or kinesthetic, and those who assessed brain hemispheric preference would only concentrate on the differences between the right and left sides of the brain, I had not found any system that combined the two. For years, I always looked at the whole picture—learning and reading comprehension style and brain hemispheric preference combined.

Working closely with a large range of learners, I saw in case after case that both assessments had to be taken into account in order to accelerate one's learning. Thus, I found there were eight broad categories and a vast difference between the way each group learned and comprehended. I have named these categories the eight superlinks to accelerated reading comprehension and learning because they provide the fastest and most effective link between the material to be learned and comprehended and our brain. The word *superlink* is used to make a distinction between the use of this method of combing both brain style and learning and reading comprehension style and the use of the method of only evaluating visual, auditory, tactile, or kinesthetic learning and reading comprehension styles without considering brain style preferences. Since the term *learning style* is used by most people excludes brain hemispheric preference, I have coined the term *superlink* because that includes both our learning and reading comprehension style preference and our brain hemispheric preference.

Eight Superlinks

After taking both assessment tests, the *Learning Style Preference Assessment*™ and the *Linksman Brain Hemispheric Preference Assessment*™ you will know your own superlink to comprehending and learning. Here are the possible main combinations, but you can be a combination of two or more of these as well:

- Visual Left-Brain
- Visual Right-Brain
- Auditory Left-Brain
- Auditory Right-Brain
- Tactile Left-Brain
- Tactile Right-Brain
- Kinesthetic Left-Brain
- Kinesthetic Right-Brain

These are the 8 superlinks to accelerated learning and reading comprehension.

Superlinks Combinations

There are people who may use a combination of these eight superlinks. If your brain hemispheric preference is integrated, your possible superlinks are:

- Visual Right- and Left-Brain
- Integrated Auditory Right- and Left-Brain
- Integrated Tactile Right- and Left-Brain
- Integrated Kinesthetic Right- and Left-Brain Integrated

The possible combinations of superlinks for mixed preferences are:

- Visual Right- and Left-Brain Mixed Preference
- Auditory Right- and Left-Brain Mixed Preference
- Tactile Right- and Left-Brain Mixed Preference
- Kinesthetic Right- and Left-Brain Mixed Preference

You may also be a combination of reading comprehension and learning styles. Some people can be visual and auditory; others can be tactile and auditory. Some are two, three, or all four learning and reading comprehension styles equally; other use all four learning and reading comprehension styles and have an integrated preference for both sides of the brain—this person would be equally using all brain modalities at once.

The following chapters contain descriptions of each type of learner and ways to use these keys to learn how to comprehend anything quickly. You will understand what each learning and reading comprehension style preference and each brain hemispheric preference means for you, and how the combination of the two—your superlink to accelerated learning and comprehending—can help you learn better, faster and more easily, and remember and comprehend better.

Suggested Note to Readers: If you plan on taking the Superlinks *Learning Style Preference Assessment*™ and the *Brain Hemispheric Preference Assessment*™ assessments, you may want to consider doing so before reading the descriptions in the rest of the book. Why? If you know the descriptions of each, some people may be predisposed to gear their answers on the assessment towards picking choices they believe will lead to their results showing them to be a particular learning and reading comprehension style and brain style, because they want to be that style, or think they are, rather than letting the results come from their unbiased choices. I have seen some cases over the years where people wanted to be identified with one particular style, and if they knew the characteristics, picked choices on the assessment that would lead their results to turn out that way. The value in taking it before knowing the specific characteristics is that it allows you to focus on each question and the choices that truly describe you, so that you see the results of your unbiased answers. However, if you prefer to read the descriptions first, and then take the assessment, you can do so, if you can attempt to answer the questions by selecting choices that describe you and not what you wish to be or what you think others want you to be.

If you wish to take the online test, go to: www.readinginstruction.com and select Superlinks Assessment. As a reader of this book, *How to Improve Reading Comprehension Quickly*, enter the special gift discount code HTLAQ for a special reduced rate for the online superlinks test. If you are a teacher, coach, trainer, employer, or someone who wishes to have students, trainees, employees, athletes, or group members take the test, you can get bulk licenses at special rates by contacting info@keyslearning.com or go to www.keystoreadingsuccess.com or www.superlinkslearning.com.

If you are reading this book to know about the different learners to help you be a better teacher, trainer, sports coach, trainer of trainers, instructor, parent, life coach, psychologist, psychiatrist, or medical doctor who deals with educational or learning and comprehension issues of your students, trainees, athletes, children, clients, or patients, or you are an employer who wants to learn how to train your employees to improve in comprehending what they are taught for doing their jobs, or you wish to improve your own reading comprehension, memory, communication, study skills, note taking, or test-taking skills and do not wish to take the assessment, you can proceed to read the rest of the book for your own specific purposes and goals.

PART 3:
WHAT IS A READING COMPREHENSION STYLE PREFERENCE AND BRAIN HEMISPHERIC PREFERENCE AND WHAT DOES YOUR BEST SUPERLINK MEAN TO IMPROVE READING COMPREHENSION QUICKLY?

CHAPTER 5:
WHAT IS A READING COMPREHENSION STYLE?

Our reading comprehension style is one part of our superlink to accelerated comprehending. Research has identified that people comprehend in different ways. We rely on all our senses to receive information from the outside world, yet, over time, many people develop one sense more than others have done and find it easier to rely on that one for comprehending new material. This is how we develop a preference for one type (or combination of several types) of reading comprehension style. If we want to comprehend something rapidly, the material needs to be presented to us in our most developed pathway to the brain—our reading comprehension style. There are four main reading comprehension style preferences: visual, auditory, tactile, and kinesthetic.

Visual learners comprehend best by seeing.

Auditory learners comprehend best by listening, hearing themselves talk, and discussing their thoughts with others.

Tactile learners comprehend best by touching or feeling sensation on their skin, by using their hands and fingers, and connecting what they learn to their sense of touch or to their feeling, either physically or emotionally.

Kinesthetic learners comprehend best by moving their large, or gross motor, muscles in space, through performing actions with their body, and by being actively involved in the learning process through simulations, role-playing, experimenting, exploration, and movement, and through participating in real-life activities.

Learners who use other senses: Though rare, there are some learners who rely on their sense of taste or smell. They can be identified because they have an acute sense of smell or taste, are sensitive to odors or tastes, and can comprehend well by involving these senses.

Reading Comprehension Style and the Brain

Brain research has advanced enough so that we have a *limited* understanding of how the brain works. Although there is still much to learn, we do know some basic principles that are relevant to understanding how we comprehend. As our brains are exposed to stimuli, new interconnections between nerve cells are created. This quality is known as *brain plasticity*. The more stimuli we receive, the more interconnections and learning patterns are formed. Thus, as certain learning patterns become more rapid, easier, and automatic, we learn and comprehend more quickly, reinforcing the development of our best reading comprehension style. This is the essence of improving reading comprehension.

We have pathways between our senses and the brain. If over time we have relied more upon our eyes, then the passageways between the nerves in our eyes and the part of the brain that interprets visual stimulus developed more than passageways between the other senses and the brain. As a result, we find it easier to rely upon our eyes and are visual learners who comprehend best what we see. For some people, the neural connections between the ears and the part of the brain that interprets auditory stimulus is stronger; thus, they find it easier and quicker to learn through the ears and are auditory learners who comprehend best what they hear. For others, the neural passageways between the skin, hands, and fingers and the part of the brain that interprets tactile stimuli of feeling physical sensation and physiological responses to emotion has been used more and those people find it easier to learn though the sense of touch and are tactile learners who comprehend best tactilely. Some have made more use of their large motor muscles, so the neural pathways from their muscles to that part of the brain that senses body motion have become stronger and are kinesthetic learners who comprehend best what they do.

When learning and comprehending something new, we need to concentrate on assimilating the new information, process, or skill. We do not want to be encumbered by trying to learn and comprehend through a weak sensory modality, so, to accelerate learning, new information should be presented in our best reading comprehension style. If you want to develop other reading comprehension styles, it is best to do so when you are not trying to learn and comprehend new material. The basic rule of thumb is: if you want to comprehend something quickly, learn it through your preferred reading comprehension style.

Some of our tendencies are genetically inherited, some are a result of exposure to certain stimuli over a long period of time, and some develop due to one's reliance on that particular sense for survival. According to research on brain plasticity, these repeated stimuli strengthen certain passageways between one or more senses and the brain.

There are men and women who fall into each of the reading comprehension style categories. There are visual men and visual women. Similarly, there are auditory men and auditory women, tactile men and tactile women, and kinesthetic men and kinesthetic women. While certain reading comprehension styles— such as the kinesthetic, movement-oriented style—seems to be attributed in some societies erroneously more to men, while others, such as the tactile reading comprehension style in some circles seem to be erroneously attributed more to women, these stereotypes do not hold true in reality. In the past, cultural pressures may have exerted influence on members of each gender to exhibit certain behaviors, and succumbing to this pressure, over time, some members of each gender habitually began to act a certain way. Through this repetition and the brain's power of plasticity new neural patterns were charted that developed into a stronger preference for a particular reading comprehension style.

Alternatively, some people may feel it is culturally acceptable to answer a question in a certain way as they feel that is the way a member of that gender should act, but it is not really the way that an individual thinks, comprehends, and processes information in his or her brain. This underscores the importance of people who take a learning and reading comprehension style or brain style assessment test to answer as truthfully and closely as possible as to which choice describes them the best and not what they believed others want them to say.

More recently, as people of both genders are given more opportunities to engage in a wider range of experiences not limited by gender stereotypes, they will develop more along the lines of their natural way of learning and comprehending, resulting in people of both sexes developing strengths in any of the learning and reading comprehension styles and brain styles. With people being more informed about learning and reading comprehension styles and brain styles, it is hoped that parents and teachers will realize the importance of exposing the young to stimuli that develop *all* their senses, giving them an opportunity to develop their *whole* brain and make better use of their natural talents.

A question frequently raised is: Since traditional schools teach people mostly through the visual and auditory sense, wouldn't all learners develop into visual and auditory learners? The answer can best be understood by a similar question: If you are right- handed, wouldn't you become left-handed if you were forced to use only the left hand in school? Think of what that would be like. You could *force* yourself to use the left hand but you would be slower, more conscious of the motions of writing than to doing the actual work, and it might take you years to become as proficient with your left hand as you are with your right hand. (The same situation would be applicable if schools were to make left-handed people write with their right hand.) It may take you the same number of years to develop your non- dominant hand as it took to become automatic with your dominant hand, putting you several years back in development of skills that require writing ability.

Similarly, if you were a visual, tactile, or kinesthetic learner, you could force yourself to develop your auditory learning and reading comprehension style, but during the years you were developing it you would struggle with material presented auditorially, putting you at a disadvantage in that environment. The same holds true for forcing auditory, tactile, or kinesthetic learners into a visual environment. When learning something new, you naturally want to use your most comfortable sense to accelerate progress. At other times, you can strengthen your weaker senses, and over time they will become stronger, but they will not equal your ability in your strongest sense unless you stop using it for a part of that time.

The Four Types of Reading Comprehension Styles

While each learner is unique, people who have the same reading comprehension style share some similar characteristics. In the following chapters on the eight superlinks, each reading comprehension style will be described so you can understand yourself and others.

If you have already taken the superlinks assessment test (see the back of the book for information on where to go to take it), you may want to begin with the chapter on your own superlink reading comprehension and learning style first, and then read descriptions of the other types. If you scored equally in several reading comprehension and learning styles, read each description of those two, three, or possibly four styles. Highlight the characteristics in each that describe your personal profile. You may also recognize qualities of other people you know.

You may find that most characteristics describe you, or only some. If the latter is true, then all the descriptions of one reading comprehension style alone may not match you completely because you use a mixture of two or more reading comprehension styles. It could be that in our jobs we develop other senses and were identifying with our work persona. If that is the case, you may find that you have several reading comprehension styles—your work style, your style when dealing with other people, and the style you are at heart. Although we may be strong in one reading comprehension style, this does not mean we neglect to use other styles in different situations. Thus, you will need to read the characteristics of each to see which portions in combination apply to you. Establishing the accurate combination is important, so when you get to the learning activities, strategies, and practice activities in the book, you employ the ones that match your combination of styles. The descriptions are not meant to be a system for labeling people for all times; rather, they allow us to form a profile of ourselves and help us communicate better and comprehend more easily and rapidly. The chapters on the eight superlinks fully describe the combinations of reading comprehension and learning style plus brain hemispheric preference and its application to improve comprehension for us so we can improve in reading, study skills, note taking, and test- taking skills to comprehend any subject quickly.

CHAPTER 6:
WHAT IS A BRAIN HEMISPHERIC PREFERENCE?

The brain is divided into two hemispheres or halves—the right hemisphere and the left hemisphere. While we all use both sides of the brain, many people process and store information using functions on one side more than the other, exhibiting a *brain hemispheric preference*. A preference for one side of the brain develops when we use particular neural pathways more, developing them to a higher degree; we become more skilled in using that hemisphere. It is not that we are incapable of using the other side of the brain, but when we use one half more, over time it feels more comfortable and natural to use.

When people receive instruction in a way that does not match their brain hemispheric preference they may take longer to learn, they may struggle, or even fail. However, when we communicate in the way that matches our brain hemispheric preference, we learn and comprehend more easily and quickly.

Scientists have helped us understand some of the characteristics of the right and left sides of the brain.

Each side looks at life differently. Thus, someone who processes and comprehends mostly through the right side of the brain will experience an event or situation differently from one who processes and comprehends mostly through the left side of the brain.

Our brain hemispheric preference is not a conscious choice, but we may grow up using mostly one side for many tasks. As children, we may have been exposed to many linear tasks, so our brain had enough stimuli to develop neural pathways that support linear thinking, referred to as left-brain thinking. Or, we may have been exposed to many holistic and global experiences, stimulating the development of global thinking, referred to as right brain thinking.

Neither side of the brain is superior to the other; they merely do different tasks important for survival.

Ideally, people should be able to use both sides of their brain equally well. Unfortunately, this information on brain hemispheric preference which has been known to researchers for decades has still not filtered down to everyone engaged in teaching and training, whether parents, teachers, instructors, sports or athletic coaches, trainers, or employers. Left to chance, some people might end up using one side more than the other and relying on that side for all tasks, even those more appropriately handled by the other side. This is why many people have difficulty learning and comprehending, or they find it takes them a long time to comprehend. While waiting for educational systems to use these new reading comprehension methods that can train all students to engage both hemispheres of the brain, we need to find ways to deal with the struggles of students who have mostly developed one side of their brain through their life experiences yet are being taught through methods targeting their less developed or less preferred side of their brain. Thus, if you have favored one side of the brain for most tasks, in this book, *How to Improve Reading Comprehension Quickly by Knowing Your Personal Reading Comprehension Style: Quick, Easy Tips to Improve Comprehension through the Brain's Fastest Superlinks Learning Style*, you will learn techniques to adapt any learning situation to be compatible with your brain's reading comprehension style preference.

Can we develop the other side of our brain if we have a preference? Yes, according to research into brain plasticity, we can, but it takes time, although the process is accelerated when learning through one's superlinks reading comprehension and learning style and brain style. Everyone has had a certain number of years learning and comprehending through one side of the brain, and you can calculate how long it may take to balance that by developing the other side. In the meantime, through your Superlinks reading comprehension and learning style and brain style preference, you can use it to your advantage to improve reading comprehension by having material presented to you in a way that is compatible with the way your brain comprehends. The rule is: learn and comprehend something new through your preferred side. When not learning, develop the undeveloped side of the brain.

While scientists are still mapping the brain and have not yet completed work that will give us a fuller understanding of how the entire brain works, we know a great deal and can apply these findings to the field of improving reading comprehension.

Learning and Reading Comprehension Style and Brain Hemispheric Preference

Learning and reading comprehension style relates to the different ways of inputting or receiving and comprehending material from the world and conveying those messages from our senses to the brain. Brain hemispheric preference deals with what we do with the data—how we process or think about, comprehend, remember, and store it once information reaches the brain.

The sensory data from our eyes, ears, sense of touch, or the muscles of our body can be channeled to the right side or left side of the brain. Each side processes, comprehends, and stores the information in different ways. It is essential to know these differences to learn how to improve reading comprehension quickly.

Some educators focus only on using learning styles when teaching, while others focus only on using brain hemispheric preference. To have a total picture of the way people need to learn, a blending of both is required; thus, the development of the concept of a superlink: learning and reading comprehension style *plus* brain hemispheric preference. It is more effective to know both our best learning and reading comprehension style and our brain hemispheric preference to improve our reading comprehension.

Differences between the Left and Right Hemispheres

Processing Information: Symbolically versus Sensorially

One difference in the way the sides of the brain process and comprehend is that the left side processes and comprehends data symbolically in the form of letters, numbers, words, and abstract ideas, and the right side processes and comprehends data in a sensory way, perceiving the world through the senses without words.

The left hemisphere allows human beings to have the gift of language. Without language, we would only perceive what we see, hear, taste, smell, and touch, and our movements, without words. We would not be able to talk about our experiences or communicate them to others. In most people, the left side of the brain handles language, although there are exceptions: One report states that in five percent of right-handed people and thirty percent of left-handed people, the speech area is in the right hemisphere of the brain. (From *The Brain: A Neuroscience Primer*, 2nd Edition, by Richard F. Thompson. New York: W.H. Freeman and Co., 1993, p. 397). Think of the hemisphere in which our speech and language center is located as a built-in translator that takes whatever happens and puts words or numbers to it.

The right side of the brain processes and comprehends information without language. It perceives sensation of sight, touch, smell, taste, movement, and the sounds of the human voice, music, and nature without putting words or labels to the experience. It perceives life as a movie without words.

Although everyone processes language, the difference is that some people *first* process everything into words and language, while other people *first* perceive the event as a pure sensory experience without words. As the material is processed and recalled in your mind, you can think about it either in words, as if a dialogue were going on in your head, or you can think about it in sensory images full of sight, sound, smell, taste, and touch, as well as movement, without words. If you wonder how this is possible, think of a time when you saw someone you knew but could not remember his or her name. You tried so hard to remember but drew a blank—yet you were sure you knew the person. This is an example of how the right brain functions—without words.

This information is critical in terms of improving reading comprehension. Why? If someone processes information and comprehends in symbols such as words, he or she will respond better to being taught in terms of words and language. If someone processes and comprehends information in sensory images, he or she will respond better to being taught in terms of sensory images and experiences. When we match the presentation of new material to our brain hemispheric preference, comprehending it is easier. When we do not do this, we may struggle with comprehending new material or may not comprehend the material at all.

This does not mean none of us use both sides of the brain to process and comprehend information. All who have both sides of their brain intact can process and comprehend words and sensory images, blending the two together to learn and perform different tasks. The difference is that when we are learning something new for the first time, we tend to process and comprehend the new material through our preferred brain hemisphere. If we receive data through our preferred side of the brain, it is more automatic, natural, and easier for us to improve our reading comprehension.

Storing Information: Step-by-Step or Simultaneously

When we learn something new, we also will find it easier if the material is presented in a way that matches the way we *store* and *comprehend* information. The left side of the brain stores and comprehends it in a sequential, step- by-step order. The left side absorbs and comprehends information in a linear order, bit by bit, one piece at a time. It has difficulty getting the big picture unless information is presented sequentially. The right side of the brain stores and comprehends information in a simultaneous, global way; it sees the whole picture or main idea at once. It has difficulty receiving and comprehending information in a step-by-step way unless it gets the big picture. Both sides of the brain are equally important, have their role to play in human life, and must work together.

Are there people who can store and comprehend the information both ways? Yes. These people have developed the use of both sides of the brain. They are equally comfortable with both left-brain linear thinking and comprehending and right-brain global thinking and comprehending. Those who do not use both sides of the brain, who favor one side, need to know their preference in order to find out how to improve reading comprehension quickly.

The characteristics of both sides of the brain will be described in the chapters on the eight superlinks.

Keep in mind that few people use only one side exclusively. Thus, few people have *all* of the characteristics described for either right-brain or left- brain learners. The higher you score for a left-brain preference, the closer you come to the description of the left brain characteristics. The higher you score for a right-brain preference, the closer you will be to the description of characteristics of the right brain learner.

If you use both right- and left-brain functions equally, or you have a mixed preference in which you used the right side of the brain for certain tasks and the left side for others, then in the section on the eight superlinks you will need the chapters on both left-brain learners and right-brain learners because you have characteristics of both. You can highlight the aspects of each side of the brain that apply to you.

If you use both sides of the brain equally, also read Chapter 7 that describes the integrated use of both sides of your brain. If you were right-brain for certain tasks, and left-brain for others, refer to Chapter 8 for a description of the characteristics of having a mixed preference. This data is important because you are identifying how *you* need to comprehend. In the later chapters, you will be applying this information to comprehend anything quickly.

Although intuition has been traditionally considered as a function of the right side of the brain, research has not confirmed this. What is perceived to be intuition could actually be a function of reading nonverbal communication, synthesizing unrelated material and events into a whole, or using one's imagination, creating thinking, or inventive abilities.

Both right-brained and left-brain people may have intuition. Future studies may reveal that intuition may be beyond the scope of the right or left hemispheres of the brain.

Each year we discover new things about the brain. As new studies arise, current data is subject to change. We must continually revise our existing knowledge as these new findings arise.

CHAPTER 7:
INTEGRATED RIGHT AND
LEFT-BRAIN LEARNERS

People who have developed the ability to use both sides of their brain to comprehend are called integrated right- and left-brain learners. They use each side appropriately for the task. For tasks more easily accomplished by the right side of the brain, they use right-brain functions.

Conversely, for tasks easily handled by the left side of the brain, they use the left side of the brain. Thus, this group of people learns easily in any kind of environment, a left- or right-brain one.

How to Develop an Integrated Brain Style through the Power of Brain Plasticity

If we develop both sides of the brain, we can make fuller use of our potential. We can continue to increase the capabilities of our brain to comprehend through the power of brain plasticity; it is never too late to work on our weaker side, although to improve reading comprehension of a subject more quickly we still want to learn through our preferred side of the brain. However, during those off-hours when we are not trying to comprehend something new, we can engage in activities that stimulate the other side of the brain. Thus, left-brain learners may want to spend some time daily in right-brain activities, and vice versa. You can read through the descriptions of the right-brain visual, auditory, tactile, and kinesthetic learners to find out what activities they do and spend some time in some of them, each day, to develop the right side of your brain to improve reading comprehension. To develop the left side of the brain, read descriptions of the left-brain visual, auditory, tactile, and kinesthetic learners and start doing left-brain activities daily.

For example, left-brain learners can develop the right side of the brain by using their left hand to draw or write (if they are not already left-handed), by playing games that involve finding missing numbers or shapes to complete a pattern, or by playing word games in which they make as many words as possible by mixing up a set of given letters. Other activities include brainstorming, inventing, or doing creative writing. Another way to develop the right side of the brain is through reading people's nonverbal expressions such as facial gestures, tones of voice, and body language, such as through turning off the sound on a DVD or television program to figure out the feelings behind the actors' and actresses' gestures. One can also take new routes to work or put away the clock and live without paying attention to time for a whole day.

Right-brain people can develop left-brain skills by using their right hand for drawing, writing, or doing activities (if they are not already right-handed). To develop the left brain's sequential, step-by-step abilities, one activity is to read a story or article and first make a right-brain mind map showing the main ideas in a large circle, with all the supporting details in smaller circles radiating as if spokes off the main ideas. Next, convert the mind map into a traditional left-brain outline format in a linear, sequential way. Other ways to develop the left side of the brain is to get a file cabinet and file your papers alphabetically or chronologically, or get a planning book or calendar, write in your appointments, and set as a goal to keep each one on time. Get a watch or beeper and program it to go off as a reminder to keep your appointments, or your to-do list, on time.

The following are characteristics of integrated left- and right-brain learners:

Understanding the World: Integrated left- and right-brain learners can think in terms of symbols and language as well as sensory experiences. When asked to see blue, they may see both the color and the letters that spell the word *blue*. They can comprehend sensory impressions as they would see a movie in their heads and can also use words and symbols to think about what they perceived. Their lives are enriched because they can think, comprehend, and process in both symbolic language such as words, symbols, and ideas, and in pictorial language and sensory input. Just as someone who is bilingual can communicate in two languages with a wider range of people, integrated learners can move easily from one environment to another and can understand people and subjects who communicate both in a right- and left-brain manner.

Comprehending Material: Integrated left- and right-brain thinkers comprehend information both simultaneously and in a step-by-step way. Thus, they can grasp the big picture in a simultaneous way, and go back and file its details in a sequential way. At times, they may work in a holistic way, thinking about the big picture. At other times, they may organize and recall their ideas or papers in a step-by-step way, alphabetically, numerically, or in some order that makes sense to them. This ability gives them the added advantage of picking the reading comprehension storage system that matches the task.

This flexibility also enables them to comprehend from both a right brain, global presentation as well as from a left-brain step-by-step linear presentation. When they present data, they do it in either a simultaneous or step-by-step way.

Sense of Time: Integrated left- and right-brain learners are aware of time. They can hide out in the right side of the brain and become oblivious of time, or they can be very scheduled when they shift over to attending to the functions of the left side of the brain. Thus, they can also pick and choose whether they will live according to a schedule or become lost in timelessness. With experience they learn which situations require a sense of time and which do not.

Visual-Spatial Relationships: The right side of the brain gives integrated left- and right-brain learners the ability to deal with visual-spatial relationships with good perception of color, shape, and design. They are aware of and comprehend the relation of objects and people in space.

Creativity and Imagination: Integrated right- and-left-brain learners can deal with two types of creativity and imagination. They can work with existing forms and objects or ideas and put them together in new ways, or they can create something new. With full use of their brain, they have a wide range of options open to them.

Communication: Integrated left- and right-brain thinkers can listen through both sides of the brain. Thus, they are hearing the words and picking up nonverbal cues as well. This makes them more aware and conscious of what is happening around them than those who only receive information through one side of the brain. Thus, integrated left- and right-brain learners are attending to the meaning of the words as well as the hidden meaning expressed by a speaker's tones of voice, or facial and body gestures. This ability allows them to communicate both articulately and empathetically with expressive gestures or tones of voice.

Whole-to-Part and Part-to-Whole Thinking: Integrated left- and right-brain learners can look at and comprehend information in both ways. They can start with the big picture and then go back and analyze the details, or they can go through the details in a linear way and then understand the sum total at the end. They can look at a book from front to back as well as back to front, or by skipping around, and be equally as happy. This fluidity of thought enables them to function in different types of learning environments with different instructors.

Synthesis vs. Analysis: Integrated left- and right- brain learners can move comfortably between analyzing and synthesizing. They can break down an idea or process into its component parts and put them back together in the same or in a new way. This makes them ideal inventors and creators. They are adept at finding new solutions to problems, creating new gadgets or inventions, finding new ways to create in the arts, or new ways to look at the world. They can look at their new synthesized creations and inventions in an analytical way so they can test it out and examine it for flaws and correct it. These people can see the total synthesized idea or product and analyze its parts to ensure that no aspect of a project or product has been left out.

The Challenges of Having an Integrated Left- and Right-Brain Style of Learning

With capabilities on both sides of the brain, the challenges of having an integrated left- and right-brain learning style means that one may feel there are two ways of thinking and comprehending inside one's head, each competing for attention. These multi-ways of thinking and comprehending make people so diverse and talented, with so many interests, that they can feel overwhelmed by their own capabilities and find it hard to prioritize. They have so much they want to do, so many people to meet and places to see, that they cannot do everything they want to do. They feel limited by the number of hours in a day and number of years in their lives. This creates its own kind of frustration, because with expanded capabilities there is so much they want to accomplish in so little time.

Benefits of Having an Integrated Left- and Right- Brain Brain Learning Style

One of the greatest plusses of having integrated use of both sides of the brain is in the area of discovery, invention, and creation. The right side of the brain can create new art forms and make new scientific discoveries and inventions, while the left side has the ability to communicate it to the world through language. There are some people who create something new but do not know how to get it across to others. Thus, it may just live and die with them. But having the ability to put one's creations or inventions into language to help others understand it, or to be able to write or speak about it in a sequential, logical way so that others can carry it further or do something with it, is an important quality to have. Thus, those with integrated use of both sides of the brain can make important contributions to humanity for others to understand and use.

Chapter 8:
Right and Left-Brain
Mixed Preferences

Some people have a right-and-left-brain mixed preference, which means that they perform some functions with one side of the brain and other functions with the others side. When they use the side of the brain that matches the task, there is no problem. Mixed left- and right-brained preference learners just need to be aware of their strengths and know how to apply them to the task.

Sometimes people with a mixed preference use one side of the brain, but not necessarily in a way that matches the task. Some people use the right side of the brain for tasks that are better performed by the left side, and vice versa. Thus, these people may find their performance is not always at its best. At worst, it creates confusion and makes comprehending a great struggle in certain situations. To provide strategies to alleviate the difficulties it may create, the rest of the chapter will focus on situations in which one is not using his or her brain in the best or most appropriate manner for the task, and what can be done about it.

Using the Right Side of the Brain for Left-Brain Tasks

Most academic subjects in schools that have been based on tasks such as reading, writing, spelling, grammar, public speaking, learning a foreign language, and doing certain math computation functions have been traditionally taught in a left-brain way, requiring understanding and comprehending abstract symbols such as numbers, letters, and words. People who use the right side of the brain when taught in this left-brain way find that it does not work and end up struggling. One reason these subjects are taught in a left-brain manner is that many people who became teachers and college instructors were people who succeeded in the educational system and could function well in this left-brain environment. Thus, when they taught the upcoming generation, they tended to use the same techniques—left-brain methods—that helped them learn and comprehend the material when they were students. However, all the subjects listed below can be taught in a right-brain manner so that right-brain people can be successful.

Right-brain techniques are presented later in this book, which gives right-brain reading comprehension skills and strategies for comprehending anything quickly.

Reading Comprehension: People with right- brain preferences read, comprehend, and remember differently than those who read with the left side of their brain. Right-brain people learn to read more easily through recognizing repeated patterns, such as phonemic or phonics patterns, in which they read, for example, at, fat, cat, hat, and so forth, and can then remember the sound that any other word with at makes when they see it in other words. They also respond to sensory words that invoke strong images processed in the right side of the brain. Thus, when they read, they are going after the big picture, the main points, the strong visual images, actions, sounds, and feelings. There is nothing wrong with reading in this manner unless you have to attend to details, abstract ideas, or small words that can change the meaning of the text. It also causes difficulties when one has to perform on an important test or task. Even if a right-brain person gets the main idea of what they read they may end up struggling with final examinations, high school or college entrance exams or placements tests (GED, ACT, SAT, GRE, etc.), certification tests, qualifying tests, or tests of reading abilities. They are placed at a disadvantage and low scores may mean anything from failure, to low self- esteem, to not getting admitted into the school of their choice and sadly, to dropping out. If a right-brain learner's career depends on certification, it could also affect his or her future. There are two options available to right-brain people who have to perform on a left-brain reading activity or test. One is to develop their left-brain skills. The second is to convert the task into a right-brain one so as to perform well on it. Without this training, right-brain people may pass through a good portion of their lives needlessly struggling with reading, comprehension, or memory; feeling like failures; or missing many opportunities to advance themselves and their career.

Spelling: Spelling is another task that requires writing letters in order, a left-brain function. Again, those who are using the right side of the brain for spelling will often find themselves mixing up letters because the right brain does not work in sequential order. This means that they may be a good writer, but in school or job situations, people will see their poor spelling and may disregard their writing abilities. However, I have taught many right-brain people to spell using right-brain techniques.

Grammar: Poor grammar can reflect on one's writing abilities, speaking abilities, and educational background. A right-brain learner may be brilliant, but if he or she does not speak or write grammatically, others will not know the depth of his or her intelligence. Again, right-brain students again struggle and find themselves getting low test scores when it comes to tasks involving grammar even though they may have brilliant ideas, because grammar requires attention to details and sequential order. Right-brain people can use right-brain techniques, however, to master grammar.

Writing: Right-brain learners may have creative ideas, but much of writing in schools and on the job is evaluated according to left-brain rules and criteria. Thus, organization and logical structure, writing ideas in sequence, correct sentence structure, and correct use of the mechanics of writing are left-brain functions. Right- brain people can become excellent writers by using right- brain techniques to master this left-brain skill.

Foreign Language: Foreign language studies require success in reading, writing, spelling, speaking, and grammar. It also requires the storage of two languages in the brain. People who use the right side of the brain to learn a foreign language may find themselves struggling with certain left-brain tasks. Thus, for example, if one wants to learn how to comprehend Spanish quickly, or learn how to understand French or German or any other language quickly, knowing how to use right-brain techniques can help with mastering left- brain skills.

Math: Certain math tasks pose another problem for people who use the right side of the brain. Many math problems can be done with right-brain techniques. Right-brain learners can grasp the whole picture, identifying patterns, and see interconnections. But when the task is presented in a text that requires reading instructions or word problems that must be solved through a step-by-step method, right-brain learners tend to struggle. Even when they can get the correct answer for a problem, they often do not get credit because they did not write how they got the results in a left-brain detailed and sequential way. Often, they are penalized for being unable to explain, in words, how they arrived at an answer.

Sometimes people with a strong right-brain preference may transpose numbers. They know what number they are writing, but when they write, two numbers often come out transposed or totally backward. This happens because the right side of the brain sees the whole number simultaneously, while it is the left side of the brain that puts the digits in order. When a right-brain person does not take the time to double-check a number, it may come out mixed up. Thus, tasks involving accuracy of computation may suffer. Through using right-brain techniques a right-brain learner can master those tasks in math that require left-brain processes.

Jobs: Many jobs require attention to order and detail such as computer programming, accounting, being a bank teller or a cashier, engineering, or proofreading, to name a few. People who have a mixed preference should be aware that they might need to use the left side of the brain to perform left-brain tasks or use right-brain adaptations for the left-brain task.

Right brain adaptations are given later in this book, which focus on learning by using your best Superlink reading comprehension and learning style and brain style to succeed.

Using the Left Side of the Brain for Right-Brain Tasks

When someone with a mixed left- and right-brain preference has been in the habit of using the left side of the brain to perform right-brain tasks, they may struggle just as those who use the right side of the brain do when performing left-brain tasks. Here are some situations in which using the left side of the brain may impede performance of a right-brain task.

In offices or planning sessions, brainstorming is often a desirable way to generate ideas and solutions for problems. The session requires letting one's mind stay open to various possibilities. It is a time in which suggestions on the floor can trigger other associations and ideas. Someone with a mixed left- and right-brain preference may end up engaging the left side of the brain and hindering the brainstorming session. Instead of staying open to all possible suggestions, the left-brainer will begin judging and analyzing each suggestion in a microscopic way, arguing why it would or would not work. The brainstorming session is not the time for judging and evaluating the details of each idea.

Interrupting a right-brain brainstorming session—a right-brain task—can bog down the process and stop the free- flow of ideas needed to find solutions. The left side of the brain needs to reserve its analytical abilities for a later time, after the brainstorming is over, when the specific suggestions are looked at for their practicality.

In tasks such as art, music, new product design, movie production, science and technology, or advertising, which involve creating or inventing something new, left-brain learners may have a hard time. They are stuck with the ideas and concepts they already know and cannot make a leap into the new and unknown. They would rather produce a step-by-step instruction manual of a process they know than explore unknown territory. They would rather be told what to do or follow directions than have the freedom to create anything they want. They need to learn to develop the right side of the brain's simultaneous thinking to help them with new ideas, make new connections, and imagine new possibilities. They must adapt the right-brain task to the left side of the brain and use their own step-by-step approach to come up with new ideas, or develop the right side of their brain.

Many tasks require the right side of the brain.

People with mixed preferences may be using the left side for tasks that would be better serviced by the right side of the brain. They, too, need to know which side is appropriate for which task so they can use that side appropriately. Left-brain adaptations are given later in this book, which focuses on techniques for comprehending by using your best Superlink reading comprehension and learning style and brain style to improve reading comprehension to master any subject.

Mistaken Identity: Is it a Learning Disability or Just Not Matching the Side of the Brain to a Task?

Many people grow up thinking they have a reading comprehension or learning problem or a learning disability when in fact they are just using the wrong techniques to learn. Even today there are thousands of students who are classified as learning disabled or having problems with reading comprehension when, in fact, a task is not presented in a way that is compatible with their brain hemispheric preference, or they have not been taught how to use the side of the brain that matches the task. A learning disability is a dysfunction of the central nervous system, which means there is impairment in the circuitry between the senses, the nervous system, and the brain. This impairment can be thought of as a short circuit in the nervous system that scrambles a message as it travels from the senses to the brain and back to the senses. This situation does not apply to someone with a mixed preference who has no central nervous system dysfunction, but who has simply not been taught how to use the right side of the brain for right-brain tasks or the left side of the brain for left-brain tasks. Someone with a mixed preference may appear to make the same mistake as someone with a learning disability, but there is a world of difference. The learning-disabled person has damage to the central nervous system which to date is not repairable (but science may find a way to repair it in the future). Thus, no matter how many times they do the same task they will not get it. They have to learn how to accomplish the task using different sensory modalities or techniques. Someone with a mixed left- and right-brain preference can learn how to use the other side of the brain or can convert the task to match the side of the brain for which a preference is shown. It is not a question of damage, but one of usage. They have been using one side of the brain since childhood causing it to develop more neural connections, resulting in making that side more efficient and rapid. The other side of the brain also can be developed, or the task can be restructured to match the preferred side.

Many people with a mixed left- and right-brain preference use each side of the brain inappropriately for certain tasks and thus may have grown up thinking there was something wrong with them or their ability to comprehend. This may affect their self-esteem and their motivation to succeed, and they may have actually dropped out of school or not continued on to higher education thinking there was something wrong to them.

Only as an adult do many people with mixed preference discover that they are not dumb or stupid, or lack good reading comprehension, but that the system they used failed them. They discover that when the instruction matches their reading comprehension and learning style and brain style they are excellent learners. It is only the approach used during their school career that was wrong for their learning style and brain style preference, and with a new approach they can finally feel success. Later in this book you will learn how to convert the language of each side of the brain into the other as a way to make reading comprehension skills easier and faster.

PART 4:
YOUR SUPERLINK TO IMPROVE YOUR READING COMPREHENSION TO LEARN ANY SUBJECT QUICKLY

CHAPTER 9:

CREATE YOUR PERSONAL SUPERLINK READING COMPREHENSION AND LEARNING STYLE AND BRAIN STYLE PROFILE

As you read about the eight superlinks in the following chapters, you will learn about your own reading comprehension superlink and form a profile of how you comprehend. You should jot down information as you read about your superlink or combination of reading comprehension and learning links in the next eight chapters. As you advance further in the book, you will use this data, applying this knowledge to improve reading comprehension of any subject quickly.

You may find that the chapter on your own superlink describes you completely. If you are a combination of two or more reading comprehension and learning styles, you may also discover that there are portions of several chapters that accurately describe you. This means that your personal profile will contain reading comprehension and learning strategies suited for you from a combination of your superlinks reading comprehension and learning and brain styles. For example, you may have found that you are a combination of two superlinks: tactile left brain and visual left brain. Thus, your personal profile will contain portions of those two chapters.

Since we use each of our senses and both sides of our brain to varying degrees, many combinations of superlinks are possible. Do not feel you have to fit precisely into one category. You may comprehend through a combination of several superlinks reading comprehension and learning styles. Some people may be fortunate enough to have developed their whole brain and find that all eight reading comprehension and learning links fit them!

The descriptions of each superlink given in the next eight chapters are not meant to restrict options for people or form stereotypes. Anyone with any reading comprehension and learning and brain style can function well at any task and in any job either by adapting to the situation, by approaching the job in a different way, or bringing his or her own unique perspective to it.

If you find that you use a combination of superlinks, pick out the portions from each superlink chapter that apply to you and take notes on that portion. The essential point is that you know what *your* particular combination means for *your* reading comprehension, and know how *you* can use it to improve reading comprehension and apply it to any subject such as memory, study skills, note taking, and test taking skills. In this way, you will have in hand your own personal profile to refer to as you move through the rest of this book.

Directions: If you have taken the Superlinks Learning Style and Brain Hemispheric Preference assessments, and know your superlink style, you can go right to your chapter or chapters related to you. Alternatively, if you did not take the Superlinks assessment, you can still read through all the chapters on each superlink in this book and as you find one or more that fit you, highlight, or take notes on the portions of each that describe how you need to comprehend. This will give you an actionable plan to improve your reading comprehension in any subject.

CHAPTER 10:
WHAT IS A VISUAL LEFT-BRAIN LEARNER AND HOW TO IMPROVE READING COMPREHENSION QUICKLY?

What is a Visual Left-Brain Learner?

Visual left-brain learners take in information through their eyes and comprehend and remember by converting it into symbols or language, such as letters, numbers, words, or ideas. Although they are sensitive to their visual environment, they pay particular attention to printed matter—letters, words, or numbers. They mentally label this sensory information with names and words. They think, comprehend, and remember in a step- by-step way, attending to one detail at a time, and file data in a systematic way, whether alphabetically, numerically, or chronologically.

Since they like to stay organized, they are often engaged in organizing materials involving words and numbers. They may spend time filing their papers, organizing phone numbers and addresses, keeping their finances up to date, paying bills, doing budgets, scheduling appointments in their offices or homes, keeping up with correspondence, programming their computers, doing spreadsheets, or making sure birthday and anniversary cards are mailed out on time. They may find organized and efficient ways for setting up accounting, payroll, record keeping, or bookkeeping systems.

To keep their life in order, they may make charts and graphs. They are good at keeping company records, archiving, setting appointments, making chronologies and timelines, keeping timetables and scheduling, and other such tasks. They do not miss a detail and seldom miss an appointment, as long as it is written so they can see it.

When they are traveling, they plan everything they are going to see in detail in advance. They collect travel brochures, schedules, and information and make reservations far in advance. They like to stick to their planned schedules and feel uncomfortable when anything interferes with anything that they have already visualized and planned in their minds.

How Visual Left-Brain Learners Can Improve Reading Comprehension to Accelerate Learning

Visual left-brain people can improve reading comprehension to accelerate their learning by reading and seeing visual materials in the form of language: letters, words, and numbers. They also need eye contact with a speaker. They comprehend any subject more quickly through reading books and study guides if the information is organized and clearly written in step-by-step order. To learn a language they need to see a vocabulary word, its definition, and visual clues for its pronunciation. To learn math they need to read step-by- step instructions showing them how to do a problem.

They tend to be accurate with mathematical calculations. Self-study programs that require reading are excellent for them.

Visual left-brain learners learn through the written word, whether through physically printed versions, eBooks, or digital downloads. They learn well through seeing books, magazines, journals, newspapers, technical manuals, guidebooks, instruction books, or power point presentations or viewing other media that has printed words presented through the computer, DVDs with textual captions, CDs or audio downloads with accompanying printed text manuals. Reading tables, graphs, charts, and posters are helpful. Written communication is a way to get a message across to them. They are quicker at responding to text messages, social media posts or blogs, E-mail, faxes, written directions, memos, or letters than to phone calls or verbal communications. Computer programs and electronic communication networks that require reading texts with step-by-step detailed instructions are ideal for visual left- brain learners.

Visual left-brain people can study with music, noise, or talking in the background because they are so focused visually that they can tune out those distractions.

Due to their keen sensitivity to visual stimuli, they are bothered by visual clutter or disorganization in print material. They comprehend what they have seen and can spot whether print looks right to them. It is as if they have an automatic spell checker in their brain. They make excellent proofreaders and copyeditors. They can also spot errors in numerical information such as financial reports, budgets, paychecks, tax returns, restaurant checks, or spreadsheets. These are the people who will take a red pen to circle other people's errors. (It might have been a visual left-brain person who invented proofreader's markings!)

They can learn and comprehend the rules of writing, grammar, punctuation, and spelling if the material is presented in order with rules and formulas printed out. They can visually recall examples they see in a textbook. They need everything in their visual environment to look right, especially printed material.

How-to, step-by-step books and guides written in a clear, sequential manner improve their comprehension and memory to accelerate the visual left-brain person's learning. They can learn how to fix a motor, cook a meal, build an addition to a home, or run a business by reading about it rather than merely observing it.

When working on projects or solving problems, visual left-brain learners should outline or sequentially list the steps they need to do to reach the solution so they can *see* their plan on paper, and make sure they have everything they need to carry out each part of the task.

Visual left-brain people can make excellent administrators and managers because they are extremely organized and can see a task through to completion.

Visual left-brain learners like to learn according to a schedule and deadlines. Keeping an organizer, calendar, or schedule book or software is ideal for them so they can see their schedule.

To improve reading, visual left-brain learners must visualize the words and details they read. Although reading words can be taught through any superlinks style, traditionally it has been taught as a visual, sequential activity based on interpreting symbols, making reading easy for visual left-brain people because they process and organize information that way. As they read, they visually record every word in their brain in order and can recall the material when questioned. Thus, they tend to do well on tests based on memorization of reading material. Visual left-brain learners are good test takers if they have study guides, notes, textbooks, or test prep books from which to study. For example, as students they need ACT, SAT, or High School Placement Test prep books and college or career prep study guides with text to do practice reading tests so they can *see* what the tests will look like. Some visual left- brain learners are like walking encyclopedias. Ask them to find a fact and they will not only recall what book they read it in, but where in the book they saw it and what visual material surrounded what they read. They are good at skimming to find needed data.

They often read as if they were a computer spelling or fact checker. They will immediately notice that something looks wrong or does not match the original data. This makes them careful readers of details, either words or numbers.

Because visual left-brain learners focus well on details, their learning is slowed down when they have to condense or summarize the gist of what they read to get the main idea. Thus, they do better on recall of facts they read than on getting the big picture or making inferences, since these are unstated and they have not *seen* them written in the text.

In the work force, dealing with print material, either in words or in numbers, is ideal for them. In the world of words, they can be found in: administration, management, office work such as preparing reports, filing, assistant work, scheduling, appointment setting, areas dealing with time-management and efficiency, publishing, writing, editing, proofreading, teaching, research in any field, library work, writing copy for advertising, marketing or sales, writing technical and instructional manuals, reviews and literary criticism, and so on. In the world of numbers they can be found in accounting, business, finance, stock brokerages, tax specialization, banking, budgeting, economics, financial planning, insurance, payroll, teaching mathematics, statistics, evaluation and measurement, market research, and computer programming.

In any career, such as medicine, law, engineering, IT, social services, education, or running a business, there are numerous tasks involving sequential thinking, which left-brain visual people find matches how they work best.

Adapting Instruction to a Visual Left-Brain Learning Style to Improve Reading Comprehension

Because visual-left brain learners focus well on details, they should ask for instruction in the form of outlines, study guides, or notes in sequential order on a white board, power point presentation, online lesson, or paper. In this way, they can see what is important, read along, or organize the information in their mind. They can improve their study skills by taking notes on what they read. If the instructor is lecturing, they can take dictation in a sequential organized way, such as by outlining or making a graphic organizer, so later they can *see* their notes or visualize it in their mind. They may need to find their own sequentially written books and materials that correspond with the subject in order to learn it quickly on their own.

CHAPTER 11:
WHAT IS A VISUAL RIGHT-BRAIN LEARNER AND HOW TO IMPROVE READING COMPREHENSION QUICKLY?

What Is a Visual Right Brain Learner?

To learn and comprehend quickly, visual right-brain learners take in information through their eyes and comprehend and remember best in the form of images, pictures, graphics, colors, shapes, faces, designs, sizes, and spatial relations. They process and think about visual stimuli in a simultaneous or global way, seeing the whole picture at once. Only after they grasp the big picture can they focus on its details.

Visual right-brain learners are attuned to the way things look and are bothered by visual clutter. They notice when the colors in a room do not match or if an object is out of place. They make good interior decorators, and with their keen sense of visual balance and design they have a good eye for what accessories go together in a room. They can rearrange a room until it looks visually pleasing. This same sensitivity makes them notice how people look and dress. They like clothes that look good and use their great eye for color and design to select matching clothes and accessories. They enjoy having their own clothes, skin, hair, or face look good as well as making others look good. Some may tell others when their hair is out of place, their tie does not match the suit, or a button is open. They are so keenly aware of how things look they can become distracted unless the disturbing visual appearance is fixed.

They like to produce work that looks visually appealing in design and color. These are the people to whom others come for attractive presentation packets, color graphics, attractively bound reports, and visual aids. Visual right-brain learners are the ones who beautify the world. They will hang paintings in a room, keep attractive posters or art around the office, and bring in the flower arrangements. People call on them to decorate the office for the staff party.

They may like going to art galleries, photo exhibits, fashion shows, or auto shows, or going sightseeing. They may get pleasure from looking at beautiful homes, gardens, cars, boats, horse or animal shows—anything that can be seen. They may enjoy the visuals of the theater, a circus, a museum, a zoo, a park, gardens, or amusement or theme parks with fascinating sights to see.

While they do not keep their things in an organized, linear way like their left-brain counterparts do, they want their visual surroundings to be appealing and will find a way to keep their things in an attractive way. Although they may not be from the filers, they will have attractive organizers such as colorful boxes, stylish containers, decorative pencil holders, and storage units for their belongings, even if within these containers, its contents are not organized sequentially.

Visual right-brain learners go with the flow and end up being in the flow, often becoming so absorbed in their visual projects that they lose track of time. Thus, they can start and finish work on their own time according to the demands of the project rather than the clock.

The best way for visual right-brain learners to improve reading comprehension to learn anything quickly is by using visual aids with graphic and pictorial content that allows them to see the big picture. They learn from or comprehend text or numbers better if they are presented using color, shape, design, special calligraphy, or an artistic font.

Many visual-right learners do not respond to verbal instructions and will find it difficult until given visual directions on paper with pictorial images, diagrams, or charts. Pure lecture does not work because they have to work hard at concentrating on auditory stimuli. When they can see a speaker, graphics, and visual aids, their best learning modality is open. To comprehend verbal lectures or oral communication, visual right-brain learners need to receive these coupled with visual stimuli. They learn and comprehend better by having eye contact with a speaker rather than listening to an audiotaped lecture, but the speaker must also give them something to look at in pictorial form.

If they do not have anything to look at and find themselves in an auditory teaching situation, visual right- brain learners can adapt by listening to the descriptive words in the lecture so they can paint a mental picture for themselves. They will have a hard time understanding what others are saying unless they are provided with descriptions of color, size, or shape to visualize in their mind.

Visual right-brain learners need to see visual aids such as graphics and pictures found in printed or digital books or eBooks, magazines, newspapers, hand-outs, Power Point presentations, online lessons, notes on a flip chart, white board, or chalkboard. It helps for them to see colorful posters, artwork, charts, maps, diagrams, graphs, visual displays, or overheads. They require illustrations, pictures, drawings, paintings, photographs, slide shows, DVDs, television, movies, live examples, real-life objects, demonstrations, and enactments with visual and scenic imagery, so they can see what you are talking about to help them understand and learn. They like computer programs or apps with good graphics and visual images that operate using icons and pictorial directions, rather than detailed, sequential directions.

When describing events or experiences from the past, visual right-brain learners will recall images they saw in real life, movies, photographs, and videos, the surroundings, and what people looked like. They are great at spotting famous personalities and people they know in different contexts by matching visual features.

Visual right-brain learners need to see objects or pictures of what you want them to do. Draw a garbage can or a broom if you want your teens to take out the trash or sweep their room. Hang posters and charts with pictorial diagrams of the steps to follow as visual reminders of your instructions. When explaining a medical procedure, doctors and dentists should give visual right-brain patients a simple pictorial chart or diagram with few words in which everything can be seen on one page. Just writing the words will not get it across to them unless there is a picture with it.

It is easier for them to do math problems when there is a photograph or pictorial image to accompany the problem as an example. If you are multiplying 24 x 3, they want to see a picture of twenty-four people each holding three slices of pizza.

Using intuition, experimentation, and discovery, they can uncover new ways to do things and find solutions for problems. They make associations easily and one image will bring others to mind. This makes them good at learning through brainstorming or making connections. Since they think things through in a simultaneous way, before starting a project, they first need to know the end product, goal, or bottom line. Once they see the big picture, the connection between every part makes sense to them. After they see the big picture, they are impatient with step-by-step directions and want to jump in and figure it for themselves as they do it.

Visual right-brain people can improve their reading comprehension by converting every word of text into images so they can see what they are reading in their head. This dramatically improves their reading comprehension. It is hard for the visual right-brain learner to grasp words that do not invoke images, such as articles like *a* and *the*, verb tenses, or prepositions. Many tend to focus on words that can be pictured and skip over these small abstract words that cannot be pictured, like *the*, *that*, or *and*, or substituting *the* for *a*, or vice versa. Thus, on a test, they often score higher on questions that contain visual imagery and lower on those that cannot be visualized. If they need to pass an examination or master abstract material, they need to develop the right-brain technique for visualizing everything, even abstract words.

They prefer books that use descriptive words that help them paint a picture in their mind as well as books with illustrations, graphics, photographs, and other visual aids. They do not like detailed, sequential books, but those that get to the point with images, people, and happenings they can see. To accelerate learning, they need to select books that give a global overview and are supplemented by graphics and pictorial images to increase understanding.

In the work force, you may find visual right-brain people engaged in the fine arts or graphic design. With their expert eye, they may be artists, illustrators, painters, sculptors, jewelry makers, clothing designers, fashion illustrators, interior decorators, beauticians, aestheticians, cosmetologists, or hair stylists. They may be involved with graphic arts, computer graphics, and commercial illustration, advertising, or designing posters, brochures, sales pieces, or billboards. In the publishing world, they may be the art directors, children's book illustrators, the layout and graphic designers, and those that make beautiful books. They make good photographers and you will find their work beautifying magazines, books, brochures, booklets, and other print or digital media.

Other activities in which they may find enjoyment are floral arranging, landscaping, or architecture. They want their visual surroundings to be beautiful. They may be the ones to design stationery, greeting cards, or new forms of calligraphy or typography fonts.

As engineers they want to design buildings, structures, or transportation vehicles that look good. They make good car designers, coming up with new sleek, beautiful models.

If involved in others fields, such as medicine, law, education, the sciences, social service, businesses, sales, finance, marketing, sports, the performing arts, music, and so on, they will learn best through visual right-brain strategies and also bring a sense of color, design, artistic sensibility, and beauty to whatever endeavor in which they engage.

Visual right-brain learners need to ask instructors to provide visual images showing the global overview. They need to see the big picture using pictorial images, mind maps, real-life objects or demonstrations, or find their own visual materials. Since auditory presentations are difficult for visual right-brain learners, they need to see a) a written copy of a lecture; or b) do their own note taking so they can read at their own pace, converting each word into a mental image; a colorful illustration; a mind map of the main topic, its details, and their interconnections; or words and numbers written in colorful, decorative calligraphy or design so they can *see* the material.

CHAPTER 12:
WHAT IS AN AUDITORY LEFT-BRAIN LEARNER AND HOW TO IMPROVE READING COMPREHENSION QUICKLY?

What Is An Auditory Left-Brain Learner?

An auditory left-brain learner learns and comprehends best and more quickly by hearing the new material presented in the form of language, either words or numbers, in a detailed, step-by-step way. They also think by speaking their thoughts aloud and conversing aloud with others. They work well with accurate data, facts, figures, and statistics and can make excellent researchers, often backing up their lectures and presentations, with information that supports their topic and gets their ideas across.

Auditory left-brain learners are sensitive to the quality of other people's speech, noticing mistakes in dialogue, such as grammatical and syntactical errors, poor usage of words, repetitive phrases, and poor delivery. They become uncomfortable when speakers drone on or use repetitive language, inappropriate pauses, or too many ums. Being conscious of speech, they are careful to be good speakers themselves and make great orators. They plan out and rehearse what they are going to say, making sure their sentences are grammatically correct and their language is precise and clear, with appropriate word choices. Many are conscious of timing and phrasing, pausing at the right place for added effect and modulating their voices in a way to keep their audiences engaged. They also make good editors, not for finding visual errors in spelling, but for being conscious of how the text should sound when read aloud. They enjoy collecting words and relish putting them together in interesting ways. They like fancy words, such as *cogitate* for *think*, and words that sound good and provide the closest shade of meaning.

They are great conversationalists and enjoy talking to a wide range of people. Their great auditory comprehension manifests itself in their speech when they quote other people like an automatic verbal playback system, replaying conversations almost word-for-word. They can be the life of the party with their storehouse of humorous anecdotes, interesting tidbits from current events and history, the wit and wisdom they heard from others, and their excellent verbal presentation skills.

They can relate famous quotations, jokes, riddles, tales, poetry, and lines from the classics, movies, or lectures almost verbatim.

Auditory left-brain learners need constant auditory stimulus. Unless studying, they cannot handle absolute silence. If it is too quiet, they feel uncomfortable and will provide the auditory sounds themselves so they have something to listen to by humming, singing, whistling, talking to themselves aloud, turning on a radio talk show, television, Internet webinar, teleseminar, or audiotape lecture, or calling someone on the phone. In an office or classroom, when it is too quiet, auditory people will start talking, wanting to discuss everything. They will either ask the speaker many questions or talk to people nearby. If no one will respond to them they may start talking to themselves aloud. The only time they need silence is when they are studying or reading, because music, noise, or the talking of others distracts them from hearing their own thoughts.

Even though they do not maintain steady eye contact with a speaker because when listening people's eyes tend to move left and right in the direction of their ears, they are good listeners and will ask a speaker many questions. Although their discussions can become lengthy because they speak with much sequential, analytical detail, their questions make others feel understood and appreciated.

Because auditory left-brain learners process their thoughts by speaking aloud, some have a tendency to repeat aloud what people around them say, either in their own way or a better way. To others who do not understand them, this may be annoying, but auditory left- brain people are not doing this to be rude or to one-up or put down others; they only repeat what others say because it helps them think about it more clearly. They also seem to make a running commentary on everything that is happening around them, which may sound to others as if they are criticizing or analyzing everything. While others may keep their thoughts to themselves, auditory left-brain learners tend to speak their thoughts aloud. They are not trying to be critical—it is as if a microphone were placed inside their head and others can hear their thoughts. Auditory left-brain learners may need to understand this tendency, lest they turn other people off unintentionally.

They work sequentially and keep their files and papers orderly. Some enjoy the sequential aspect of working with mathematics by doing number and logic puzzles and solving math problems in everyday life.

Some understand the highly mathematical and sequential

processes involved in economics, stocks, taxes, and finances and enjoy reading financial papers and business journals, keeping up with the stock market and the business world. They like to keep their financial records, both personal and business, straight, and like to be organized at tax time to do their returns.

Left-brain auditory people who are musically inclined enjoy listening to music and going to concerts, theater, or musicals. Reading music is easier for them because it involves converting musical sounds into symbols and vice versa. When they listen to music they are conscious of the technical aspects and analyze it according to their high standards, judging its technical execution such as the arrangement or a singer's voice quality, which makes them excellent music critics.

How an Auditory Left-Brain Learner Can Improve Reading Comprehension Quickly

Auditory left-brain learners can comprehend and learn quickly and best by listening and talking when ideas are presented sequentially. In the classroom or in seminars, they learn best through lectures, oral presentations, and discussion. They comprehend details of conversations, lists, words to a song, or anything else if it is told to them in a step-by-step way. Whether learning how to learn a language, fix a car, write a computer software program, or play a sport, they learn better by listening to directions than by watching someone else perform the task. To improve study skills and test-taking skills to comprehend material for a test, they need to hear the material, talk about it, reread it aloud, or record themselves reading aloud and then play it back several times.

They grasp the meaning of verbal communication quickly without having to convert it into pictures. They can closely follow a college lecture, a verbal training session on the job, or auditory directions, while others of different learning styles may be saying, What did the speaker say? I don't get it. Auditory left-brain people usually find others clustering around them asking them to explain announcements given over a PA system or to repeat the new policies that the boss explained at a meeting.

This group can be found attending lectures and seminars, or taking the audiotaped or guided tours through museums. Some are so absorbed in listening to a lecture during a sightseeing trip that they forget to look at the actual sights!

Auditory presentations such as audio books, webinars, teleseminars, movies, or DVDs played through digital or electronic devices or computers, or though radio or television are good learning tools for auditory- left brain learners. They may relax by listening to news or talk shows on the radio while driving, or listening to the evening news or a documentary on television or over the Internet after work. They also enjoy reading books, news magazines, newspapers, Internet articles, blogs, postings, and professional journals because when they read they hear the words in their head. Computer or digital programs with voice, verbal presentations, or text they can read aloud themselves, presented in a step-by- step way, are the best learning tools for them.

Auditory left-brain learners can comprehend better and learn well from technical manuals and instructional guides if they read them aloud. They are also good at writing them. These are the people who know how to write computer software programs or can follow the directions to set-up newly-purchased electronic or computer equipment. If you do not already have an auditory left-brain friend, you may want to search for one because these are the people who understand the way things work in this technological age, based on the language of words, numbers, and computer terminology carried out in a logical, step-by-step way.

Many enjoy history, current events, and biographies because these are sequential, chronological, and verbal genres.

They are sensitive to auditory distractions. When they are listening to a speaker, they become annoyed if anything distracts them. A passing car, a humming heater, or someone crunching chips will drive them out of their minds. Since they cannot tune out auditory distractions as visual people can, they carefully orchestrate their listening environment to hear only the speaker or only their own thoughts. They have a hard time concentrating or studying with background music and need quiet to read and study. Headphones or earplugs may help them concentrate when there is too much auditory distraction.

Many auditories enjoy debate. They work well in teams and cooperative groups that involve discussion and use this continual feedback to restructure and regroup their own thoughts.

To improve comprehension of what they read better, auditory left-brain learners need to read aloud, read softly to themselves, or hear the words in their mind. Some of them, though, if asked to read silently will automatically subvocalize by moving their lips, whisper-read, or read softly anyway. They need to stop frequently and ask themselves questions about what they read, either aloud or by hearing the answers in their head. They also need to hear what they read in a step-by-step way to grasp the material. If they read material that jumps from one idea to another without any order, they need to restructure it in their minds by asking questions in order to convert it into a step-by-step process and form an outline or study guide. They do not enjoy books that ramble on going nowhere, but those that are sequentially organized and move to a logical conclusion or resolution.

In the work force, they can be found in jobs requiring listening and talking in a step-by-step way. They may be public speakers, sales and marketing people, medical doctors, nurse practitioners, lawyers, politicians, administrators, scientists, presenters, lecturers, college professors, teachers, disc jockeys, musicians, singers, songwriters, editors, writers, poets, actors and actresses, announcers, emcees, broadcasters such as television news anchors, sportscasters, or announcers for commercials or audiobook recordings. Some who are mathematically included may become mathematicians, accountants, bookkeepers, bankers, financial planners, tax specialists, economists, and stockbrokers.

No matter what their careers, auditory left-brain people are the ones asked to do tasks that involve speaking, listening, or giving oral presentations and training to the staff, clients, or trainees, because oral presentations of words and numbers are their medium for communication with the world.

Adapting Learning to an Auditory Left-Brain Style to Improve Reading Comprehension

Auditory left-brain learners should ask an instructor to present material in an auditory, sequential way through lectures and discussion to help them comprehend better. Auditory left-brain people should use audio books or, if not available, use printed or digital books or do their own note taking in a linear manner to read aloud or into a tape recorder to hear it played back. Studying with a partner or discussion group helps them *hear* the material.

CHAPTER 13:

WHAT IS AN AUDITORY RIGHT-BRAIN LEARNER AND HOW TO IMPROVE READING COMPREHENSION QUICKLY?

What is an Auditory Right-Brain Learner?

Auditory right-brain learners comprehend and learn best through hearing and are attuned to sounds, music, rhythms, and nonverbal tones of voice, and strong sensory words that give an overview or the big picture. This group is sensitive to sounds that others do not notice, such as fans humming, cars passing, or equipment noise. Musical harmony is important to them because they are particularly bothered by any dissonant sounds. They are attracted to beautiful sounds, sweet melodies, and pleasing voices and are repelled by annoying and grating sounds such as sirens, construction drills, or irritating voices.

They enjoy traveling to get away from the dissonant sounds of a city to spend time relaxing amidst the sounds of nature in the mountains, a forest, or by the ocean. To keep the sounds at home or in their office pleasant, many have a good selection of music for background. Some enjoy environmental sound recordings such as the soothing sounds of the ocean, gentle rain, chirping birds in the forest, or running brooks.

Auditory right-brain learners have a good ear for music. They enjoy going to concerts, musicals, jazz brunches, or music clubs, or religious and social ceremonies with musical services or presentations. They can hear a tune, remember it exactly, and either sing it or use an instrument to play it perfectly by ear. Many auditory right-brain people in the music field may not have had any formal music training and cannot read music; they just make music and it sounds great.

They spend time practicing and creating their own songs and instrumentals. They may create by hearing a new song, tune, or whole symphony in their heads coming to them intuitively, and then can reproduce it with instruments or by singing. It is as if they are tapped into an internal audio player that creates new melodies and songs.

Auditory right-brainers get creative ideas for sound effects, often coming up with new types of sounds, new genres of music, new instruments, or new combinations of instruments and sounds, such as combining music and the sounds of nature.

Right-brain auditory learners feel uncomfortable with absolute silence unless listening to the silence—between words, in the pauses of songs, or in nature. But even in the silence, nature speaks to them. When not particularly listening to silence, they feel uncomfortable when there is no auditory stimulus. Thus, they will create it by turning on music, or making the auditory stimuli themselves, such as singing, humming, whistling, tapping a beat, making their mouth sound like instruments or sound effects, mimicking voices or people's accents, or doing impersonations or cartoon character's voices.

Although they do not maintain direct eye contact with a speaker, because their eyes move from side to side in the direction of their eyes, they are acutely aware of nonverbal communication and tones of voices. They can pick up on someone's negativity, hidden anger, resentment, and sarcasm.

Conversely, they can also pick up someone's sincerity and loving, caring, and kind attitude from their tone of voice and will immediately respond to that person. Others may think they are mind readers because they can grasp people's true meaning from subtle nuances of tone in face-to-face and telephone conversations, no matter what words are used to hide the speaker's feelings. Auditory right-brain people appear to be deep, not saying much, but understanding all.

They enjoy being with people who do not stress their verbal auditory system. Some like to talk a lot to friends about their interests and hobbies, getting to the main point quickly and changing topics frequently, while others like to be with people with whom they can relax, not have to talk much, and can communicate with few words or with strong sensory language.

How an Auditory Right-Brain Learner Can Improve Reading Comprehension to Learn Anything Quickly

Auditory right brain learners can improve reading comprehension to learn anything quickly by listening to sound, music, and strong sensory language that gives an overview or big picture. They comprehend better and learn from the sounds of words more than from printed text. When they are learning material for a test or speech, it is better for them to hear someone else read the material and pick it up from the other's intonation and voice quality, or to write down the information themselves and read it aloud, talk about it, or tape-record it so they can play it back slowly several times. They can comprehend and repeat words verbatim better if they are combined with music, rhymes, rhythm, catchy songs and tunes, jingles in commercials and advertisements, poetry, raps, beats, environmental sounds, or by mimicking distinctive voice qualities or accents. They comprehend a story conveyed in a musical, or the words to a song on DVD or music videos. As children, they may have learned the alphabet by singing the alphabet song or learned number facts by listening to children's songs.

Their best learning pathway is open when words and numbers are tied to music.

This group, which is not attuned to symbolic, abstract language such as letters, words, and numbers in a step-by-step presentation, does not learn well from lectures unless a person gets to the point using sensory words. They need to hear the bottom line and whole concept of how things are interrelated without going into details. When other people's conversation becomes too abstract, detailed, and sequential, some auditory right- brain learners may either cut them off and say, I get it, because they have grasped the whole idea or they tune out, drift off, hear a song in their head, hum it softly, tap the beat, or even sing it while the other person is still speaking. They will refocus on the lecture only when the speaker gets to the main point.

Live music, music recordings, Internet or multi- media presentations with music, movies, DVDs, television, computer programs, video games, and apps with good music and sound effects are the best learning materials for them. Sound makes these more enjoyable for them. Imaginative, interactive, and nonsequential computer programs and apps that can use sound effects, voice, and music are also good.

They understand better when words are tied to movies, DVDs, and real-life demonstrations because of the right brain's excellent visual-spatial memory. They can comprehend and remember better by mentally converting words into a movie in their heads, with imagined music, sound effects, and dialogue with expressive tones of voice. This association technique helps auditory right-brain learners learn how to learn languages and abstract subjects such as grammar, spelling, vocabulary, or algebra, traditionally taught in a left-brain way.

To comprehend procedures, auditory right-brain learners need to imagine each action as a movie in their heads, while discussing it aloud with sound effects or tones of voice, understanding the global overview first and then filling in the details. Their study partner should go over each step slowly and carefully with them, ask them to repeat the material back, including small, abstract words, and check their accuracy until they get it.

When writing, speaking, or reading they tend to get to the main point quickly and often leave out the unimportant, abstract words. When they express their thoughts, read, write, or spell, the right side of the brain, being global rather than sequential, does not attend to order and sometimes mixes up words, or mixes up letters when spelling. They may pop out with a word stored in memory close to the word they mean, for example, they mean to say dog, but instead say cat, because of their close association as four-legged animals. Also, they may read the first few letters of a word and intuitively try to figure out the rest of the word, thus coming out with a word that sounds close to the right one but is not correct. They get a global impression instead of reading each letter, in order.

When doing math, they understand the broad concepts or processes, but may not attend to the specific details of checking their work, doing step-by-step processes, or proving their answers. They can get an answer intuitively by finding relationships and patterns and grasping the whole process, but when it comes to the details of calculations, they may make errors. They may see a multiple-digit number simultaneously and come out with the first response that comes to mind. Thus, they may read 378 as 738 or 873. Others may mistakenly think they have dyslexia or a learning disability, but it is not—it is just that the right brain sees everything simultaneously instead of in linear order.

Since language in most people is usually located in the left hemisphere of the brain, auditory people with a right-brain preference may have difficulty with listening skills and may not be able to follow spoken language quickly. They often need directions repeated several times in order to grasp it and will ask those around them, What did the speaker say? What are the directions? Since they mostly grasp words that convey sensory stimuli they may miss some important abstract words such as not, if, after, before, and other prepositional phrases. Thus, if they hear Do not read this, they may pick up only do read this, causing them to make mistakes in school or on the job. Auditory right-brain learners need to learn some coping strategies. Those who are speaking to them should also understand that auditory right-brained people need instructions to be given slowly, one item at a time, often repeated two or three times, with sensory imagery, if possible. They need the extra milliseconds to take the words conveyed to the left side of their brain to cross over to be processed in the right side of the brain, converting each word into a sensory image, if possible with sound effects or tones of voice, and then, if a response is needed, to convert them back into words by processing them in the left side of the brain. This crossing back and forth between both hemispheres of the brain takes longer than it takes an auditory left-brain person, who hears words in the left side of the brain and formulates a response from the left side of the brain without any crossing over of the brain hemispheres.

Because they are easily distracted by sounds, auditory right-brain learners need an environment in which only one auditory stimulus is going on at once, whether it is a person speaking or music. Headphones or earplugs are good ways for them to shut out unwanted sounds when they are learning.

Auditory right-brain learners think mostly intuitively, without words. They pick up meaning from music, sounds in the environment, and people's tones of voice. Left-brain people may marvel at how someone can think and learn without words, but it is a different kind of learning—it is an instantaneous knowledge that does not require words, like two friends knowing what the other is thinking without even talking.

To improve reading comprehension, right-brain auditory learners first need an overview of the reading material. Then, as they read, they can fit all details into the whole picture. They need to imagine the text as a movie with sound effects, accents and tones of voice, feelings, and music to make the material come alive.

They can read as if they were a movie sound effects person who must add the appropriate sounds and images to a script.

When they read, they grasp the key or main words, sensory words, words that sound good to them, or words for music or sounds. Vocabulary describing sound attracts their attention. Auditory right-brain learners comprehend better when they read aloud, or, if that is disruptive to others, they should read softly or hear the words in their head. As with listening, they tend to skip abstract words that do not invoke any imagery such as articles, connecting words, prepositions, time words, conditional words, and auxiliary verbs, or they tend to substitute these words for each other. Thus, they may tend to read quickly because they skip too many of these abstract words. Also, they may read the first few letters of a word and intuitively figure out the rest of the word, thus coming out with words that sound a little like the right word, but are missing the middle or ending syllable. The right hemisphere of the brain does not pay attention to reading each letter of the word in order, one at a time. It gets an impression of the word because it sees all the letters simultaneously and says the first word that pops out, be it right or wrong.

As they are better at grasping an overview, big picture, impression, or main idea of what they are reading, they tend to miss details that may affect the meaning. On reading comprehension tests, they get the gist of what they read, but have difficulty with specific facts about time order, sequence, or detail questions.

To overcome this right-brain tendency, they need auditory right-brain techniques to get them to slow down and consciously make an effort to pay attention to directionality, such as reading words in English from left to right, letter by letter, without skipping words. By using pointers, guides, or highlighters in color as they read aloud they can monitor their progress to ensure that they read each letter of a word, in order, without skipping parts of the word and that they read each word in a passage, without skipping any. Visualization techniques help them experience what they are reading, word by word, or phrase by phrase, like hearing the sound track of a movie to make sure they do not miss anything and to help improve retention of smaller details, abstract time words, and prepositions. (Note: Auditory right-brain people do not visualize as visual right-brain people do as they are not focusing on what things look like, but they are intuitively experiencing the text with the sounds that would accompany it as if a sound track to a movie.) They can talk about what they are experiencing in their head as they do this, either to someone else or to themselves, out loud, or hear the sounds of the words inside their head, as an auditory reinforcement to what they are imagining.

In the work force, you may find auditory right- brain people in jobs that require listening to sounds, music, and nature in a global, simultaneous way. They may be musicians, songwriters, musical arrangers, conductors, members of a rock group, jazz trio or quartet, rhythm and blues group, orchestra, or band.

Auditory right-brain people are so sensitive to sound and its variations that they are the ones who make good sound mixers and sound editors for a recording studio, concert halls, or music, movie, video, or audio production company. Some may become the sound effects technician or special effects technician for a movie, television, video, or audio production company.

If they work in the fields of medicine, science, technology, social science, business, finance, education, service industries, marketing, sales, or professional services, they can learn their career or job through auditory right-brain techniques and will be contributors to making everything in their workplace sound good.

Whatever their profession is, auditory right-brain learners are low-key, laid back people who enjoy the harmony, music, and the positive vibrations that flow from people around them.

Adapting Learning to an Auditory Right-Brain Style to Improve Reading Comprehension

Auditory right-brain learners can ask instructors to enhance their lectures to aid in reading comprehension by giving the big picture or main idea first, before filling in with the details, and to use short sensory language, music, or sound effects along with images, mind maps, real-life objects, or demonstrations. Because many lectures are too fast-paced for them to follow while taking notes, they need to have a printed study guide, text, or tape recording so they can work at their own pace to convert the words into the following: a) a mental movie with images, sensory language, sound effects, and music along with their talking aloud or to themselves about what they are visualizing; b) illustrations of the information with key words highlighted in color as they talk aloud to someone else or themselves to associate the sounds of the words with the information; or c) mind maps or idea webs that show the main idea and details and their interconnections in colorful, creative ways.

They need to participate in real-life situations and find materials that give the overview or big picture using sensory words and visual aids that correspond to the subject, and work at their own pace converting it into a movie in their mind while talking about it with sound effects, rhythm, or musical tunes.

CHAPTER 14:

WHAT IS A TACTILE LEFT-BRAIN LEARNER AND HOW TO IMPROVE READING COMPREHENSION QUICKLY?

What Is a Tactile Left-Brain Learner?

Tactile left-brain learners comprehend and learn best sequentially through the symbolic language of letters, numbers, and words. They also learn and comprehend using their hands and fingers, their sense of touch, and their feelings. They often hold a pen or pencil, and write to think and listen better. If they are told to put their pen away, they will find some other object to touch or something to do with their hands.

They are sensitive to language coupled with nonverbal communication such as a speaker's facial gestures, body language, tones of voice, and mood, which makes them doubly aware of other people's messages. They maintain eye contact mostly to read a speaker's expression and then look down and away when they think. They tend to be able to articulate their own feelings well and can easily empathize with others. They often gesticulate with their hands and are generally expressive. Tactile left-brain learners are sensitive to other people's feelings and their own feelings get hurt easily. They think with their heart and express their thoughts verbally or in writing in terms of feelings. If learning material is tied to a physical or emotional sensation it will be more meaningful to them. They spend time working on relationships, being with family and loved ones, writing heartfelt letters, emails, or texts, or talking on the phone to those who are important in their life.

Tactile left-brain learners get new ideas as intuitive feelings and then conceive of a step-by-step approach for carrying them out. When ideas come, tactile left-brain people feel impelled to write them down sequentially. They may wake up in the middle of the night with an idea and have to write it immediately. They can be passionate about their ideas, and this enthusiasm rubs off on others. They are highly motivated and use their logic and ability to express their feelings in words to convince others of their ideas.

How Tactile Right-Brain Learners Can Improve Reading Comprehension to Learn Anything Quickly

Tactile left-brain learners can accelerate their reading comprehension and learning of anything quickly by participating in activities that require the use of their hands and fingers. They need to write what they see and hear in order to learn in a sequential way. They are interested in words or numbers. In seminars or lectures, they may take copious notes in a linear, sequential way, but they never need to look at them again. The act of writing or copying material from text or taking dictation from a lecture, by itself, helps their brain process information and enables them to recall it later. They also recall the order in which they wrote the notes.

Many think and listen better when they doodle, draw, or hold something in their hands. If restricted from writing in a seminar, you may see fidgety behaviors such as playing with objects, twirling pencils, tapping their fingers on their desk, or anything else they can do with their hands. Because of their left hemispheric preference, they tend to organize notes or make outlines, lists, diagrams, or charts.

For every subject they learn, they require active hands-on experiences with manipulatives or real-life objects to accompany a lecture or seminar. Once they have typed something, they will remember it. They also comprehend by constructing and building things with their hands in a linear, step-by-step way. In science, they need to not only perform the experiment (a good hands- on activity), but also write about the results. They do not comprehend as well if a teacher just shows and explains new material to them without allowing them to first write it down or guiding them in performing a task so they get a feel for doing it.

In order to comprehend, tactile left-brain learners need to use paper, notepads, blank books, journals, diaries, stationery, electronic devices such as laptops, notebooks, or tablets; pencils, pens, a stylus for electronic devices, markers, crayons, paints, sculpting materials, arts and crafts, board games, computers, sports equipment that involves the hands, musical instruments, real-life objects, manipulatives, and other hands-on materials. Sequential computer programs that allow them to type, interact with others at a feeling level, and communicate with others are ideal. Communicating with others through social media sites on the Internet, emailing, or writing text messages or blogs, allows them to use their hands and involve their feelings.

When learning material for a test, they will best comprehend the material they learned by touching, writing, drawing, or experiencing it at an emotional level. They can comprehend a subject in detail when they can associate the experience with a physical sensation or involving their feelings while learning, which makes it more meaningful and relevant to them. They can learn from movies, DVDs, videos, or books that touch their emotions and heart. Visual and auditory details can be comprehended if tied with an emotion. Thus, they will remember seeing a smile that conveys warm feelings and remember hearing words conveyed with love. When tactile children learn their language, it is the love of their parents expressed through words that helps the words sink in.

They learn well and comprehend better in a peaceful environment, such as a setting in which they can be surrounded by mountains, trees, or a lake. They need to be comfortable while studying. Since they are attuned to sensation on their skin such as hard and soft, hot and cold, rough and smooth, bodily comfort aids their ability to focus on learning. Thus, many like to stretch out on the floor, recline comfortably on a chair, or lie on a couch. They may be able to type, write, read or study with music, if it is music they like, because they focus on the feelings, not the words. The good feelings their favorite music brings help them tune out negative stimulus from others, focus on positive feelings, and stimulate them to be more productive.

They need positive feelings in order to concentrate or they may shut down. They cannot concentrate when they feel others do not like them. Negative vibrations from others, both verbal and nonverbal, need to be minimized. If they feel emotionally uncomfortable, tactile left-brain learners use language in an organized, clear way to question others about what they are really feeling based on their tones of voice and will talk with others to straighten out the situation. If they cannot talk about their feelings, they can write them as poetry, essays, journal entries, or blog posts.

Tactile left-brain learners can benefit from learning in cooperative teams or groups, if they like the people. They thrive on positive feelings from group members with whom they feel comfortable, and whose appreciative words and warmth help them work better. If their socializing distracts others, tactile left-brain people can be encouraged instead to write about their feelings Writing about their feelings and socializing with others does not hinder their ability to listen and work, but actually increases interest in their work.

To improve reading comprehension, tactile left- brain learners need to internalize what is happening.

They need to feel what the words describe and what the characters are feeling. They are bored if they cannot emotionally identify with what they are reading.

If they are reading about abstract subjects, they can personify the material, even if inanimate objects, to feel what is happening better. For example, if they are reading about a chemical reaction, they need to imagine themselves becoming one of the chemicals and experience themselves rising up as a gas. If they are reading a biography, they need to feel what the person would have lived through at a tactile and emotional level. They can actually comprehend everything they read if they convert the material into a feeling. What they do not convert into a feeling can be lost.

In whatever they read, they will also comprehend it better if they jot down their ideas as they read, in a sequential way. They may read books or novels that have depth, feeling, and a powerful message. They may read self-help and how-to books to solve a problem, to help them deal with feelings and relationships, or to learn something important for their jobs or life skills. They prefer it if these topics were written in a step-by-step, logical manner.

In the workforce, you may find tactile left-brain learners in jobs that require the use of their hands and fingers or involvement of their feelings that involve working in a step-by-step way. They tend to be structured and organized in their work.

If they go into fine arts, such as drawing, painting, or sculpting, they approach their work in a detailed way. When they draw, they tend to be good at copying what they see in detail and paying more attention to the technical aspects of the art, such as the mathematical nature of perspective or color mixing, etc. They may enter the commercial arts and do layout, design, fashion illustration, children's book illustrations, computer graphics, or advertising.

Some play instruments or write music and songs because these activities involve both their hands and fingers and the way the music touches their feelings.

Tactile left-brain learners may be involved in farming; gardening; landscaping; floral arranging; architecture; drafting; city planning; electrical engineering; designing electronic, technological, or computer equipment; technical writing; construction; building; painting; plumbing; wallpapering; the restaurant business; or cooking. When doing arts and crafts, sewing, knitting, building models, woodworking, sculpting, basket weaving, or making textiles, jewelry, or pottery, they learn by reading the instructions and working in a step-by-step way. They can express their feelings through any of the communication arts from print media to film making, photography, dance, and theater. Because they are so attuned to feelings, they also make good actors and actresses.

As writers, tactile left-brainers produce narratives, essays, journalistic forms of writing like newspaper articles, magazine articles, newsletters, website content, blogs, advertising copy, biographies, history with a humanistic approach, how-to and self-help books, and educational, informational, or technical instructions or manuals to help people do their job better. They offer clear, practical, step-by-step solutions. If they write fiction, screenplays, poetry, or children's books, they tend to learn the formulas and rules for writing in those genres. They may be involved with digital or eBook publishing and doing their writing, artwork, and layout on a computer. If they give lectures or trainings, they first write out their speech in a structured outline, and then follow the outline. They prefer to make their presentations more interactive and make only limited use of Power Point so they can make personal face-to-face connections with the attendees. They speak with passion and feeling, in a clear, logical way to get their ideas across and penetrate deep into the heart of audiences.

Many are involved in step-by-step sports that involve their hands, and learn by writing the instructions for how their body should move or the rules of the game. If someone is explaining a tennis stroke to them, they do better if they can take notes about it, think it through, feel themselves doing it first, perform it, and have a coach give feedback so they can adjust the stroke until they get it right.

Many tactile left-brain learners become involved in careers that deal with feelings, help people, or alleviate suffering, such as medicine, science, social work, education, psychology, relationship work, therapy, humanitarian projects, running social organizations or family shelters, ecology projects, working for peace, or helping the homeless, the needy, orphans and so on.

Whatever their careers, they reach others' hearts by involving their feelings and touching them in a deep way.

Adapting Learning to a Tactile Left-Brain Learning Style to Improve Reading Comprehension

Tactile left-brain learners should ask instructors to let them do note taking from a lecture or seminar or from printed outlines, study guides, or data presented in sequential order to comprehend better. For note taking sequential notes on their own, they need sequentially organized books and other written and audio-visual materials. They can talk to the instructor or co-workers about their need for positive communication and feedback. If there is no change in a negative environment, they can write their thoughts and feelings in a journal or talk to someone. They can also learn relaxation techniques and coping skills to deal with their sensitive feelings.

CHAPTER 15:
WHAT IS A TACTILE RIGHT-BRAIN LEARNER AND HOW TO IMPROVE READING COMPREHENSION QUICKLY?

What Is a Tactile Right-Brain Learner?

Tactile right-brain learners are sensitive people who tend to think globally. To improve reading comprehension to accelerate learning, tactile right-brain learners look at the big picture or overview and learn using their hands and fingers, their sense of touch, sensation on their skin, and their feelings. They use intuition, imagination, language that expresses feelings, and sensory words.

They are adept at reading nonverbal communication and also express themselves in a nonverbal way by making facial gestures or sounds of pleasure and displeasure or by gesticulating. When they speak they use strong feeling words. They are sensitive to other's feelings and their own are easily hurt. They are moved by sad or touching parts of movies and books.

Loving relationships are important to tactile right-brain learners because they need to feel good emotionally to function. They spend a great deal of time communicating, either by phone or face to face, so they can read other people's nonverbal expressions and tones of voice. Their eyes alternate between maintaining eye contact mostly to read other's expressions and looking down and away to think.

Tactile right-brain learners think with their hearts and

express their thoughts nonverbally. They receive new ideas and information intuitively or through gut feelings, as if an entire thought package comes to them as a finished product along with a strong feeling about it. They feel passionately about these ideas and can be extremely persuasive in trying to motivate others as to their value. They may not be detailed or systematic in bringing the idea into reality but often jump in and carry it out impulsively. Having the end product in mind, they will try to get there as quickly as possible without worrying about details.

Since they do not need to think in words, they can understand new information quickly because they can comprehend the whole picture instantaneously. They often startle those around them by accurately describing what the other person is thinking. They can get the gist of a two-hour lecture in moments through intuition.

Tactile right-brain learners work in an original and imaginative way. They often come up with new images and designs that no one has thought of before. As writers, they gravitate to imaginative kinds of writing. In the arts, they create new art forms or new ways of presenting old forms. They may use art to express their feelings. They may be involved with arts and crafts, painting, drawing, sculpting, sewing, knitting, textiles, pottery, basket weaving, jewelry making, or woodworking. Some like to play an instrument and create their own original and imaginative music and songs, filled with feeling. They can play by ear and pick out a tune without reading music.

Some tactile right-brain people enjoy games and sports that involve their hands. Since they do not have the patience for the constraint of organized games with long directions, rules and regulations, they prefer to play for fun. They do not necessarily play to win, but for the social contact with people they like, or because they like the feel of the game. When learning a new game, they tend to just jump in and perform it, getting a feel for it as they go along and learning by trial and error. Many prefer free-form games and sports involving tactile sensations in which they can be creative in their moves such as dance, gymnastics, ice skating, roller skating, Rollerblading, or swimming.

How Tactile Right-Brain Learners Can Improve Reading Comprehension to Learn Anything Quickly

Tactile right-brain people can improve reading comprehension to accelerate their learning quickly by involving their hands, fingers, and feelings. Since they are not attuned to symbolic language, they learn and comprehend through sensory language or nonverbal communication that gives the big picture. They learn and comprehend by drawing pictures, diagrams, illustrations, maps, and making sculptures, models, or artistic booklets.

Tactile right-brain learners comprehend by note taking through drawing but never need to look at them again. They comprehend new material better when they do note taking using calligraphy or colorful, artistically drawn letters. The act of drawing or writing artistically helps them understand and comprehend the material.

While listening to seminars, talking on the phone, or speaking to someone, they may doodle or jot down quick sketchy notes, pictorial icons, diagrams, or mind maps in a

133

way that shows the interrelationships between the ideas. They tend to write or draw in a circular way all over the page in no particular order. Since they are not auditorially attuned to abstract language, it helps if they can see visuals or graphics to copy.

To listen, comprehend, or think better, they need to do or hold something with their hands. It could be a pen, paintbrush, clay, a computer mouse, or any object. If they are told not to touch anything, they will fidget by playing with objects, tapping their fingers on their desk, playing with their hair, or anything else they can do with their hands to help them listen.

They also need the big picture, not the small details, or they will feel lost. They may become impatient with lengthy written directions, and would rather just get a feel for the project at hand. When remembering how to do a math problem they need to see and draw or write out the whole problem with the answer and all the steps mapped out. Then, they should try to do it themselves. The right side of the brain is adept at figuring out mathematical patterns just from seeing the problem and its solution and similar examples several times.

When they need to use study skills and test- taking skills to learn material for a test, tactile right-brain learners comprehend best that which they felt, touched, drew, wrote, or identified with at the level of their emotions. The subject matter or any auditory or visual material needs to be tied to their tactile sense and emotions.

Tactile right-brain people need hands-on experiences and manipulatives to learn. Lecturing or reading directions will not be as effective unless their hands can be involved. For example, writing and illustrating the table of elements can help them comprehend it. If it is not possible to use their hands, they need to use their imagination to visualize themselves doing the task with their hands and feeling the sensation in their mind.

The following materials help tactile right-brain people learn quickly: sketch pads; drawing paper; notepads; blank books; diaries; electronic devices on which to draw such as a laptop, tablet, or notebook; pencils, pens, markers, or crayons; a stylus; sculpting tools; paints; and arts and crafts materials. In math, using objects, counters, calculators, or manipulatives help them learn faster. Real-life items, such as tools and equipment from all fields, board games, sports equipment, or musical instruments can help them learn many subjects. They like the more free-flowing, nonsequential aspect of the computer offered by the use of the mouse, or user- friendly programs that require a click on an icon. Their tactile dexterity can also make them quick at typing or texting. They may also be good at computer graphics.

Tactile right-brain learners comprehend best in a positive learning environment that is physically and emotionally comfortable. Negative nonverbal communications from others need to be eliminated. Due to their sensitivity to nonverbal communication, their right brain picks up sarcastic tones, resentment, hatred, annoyance, and other negative feelings. When they hear these tones, their openness to learn shuts down. They may withdraw or respond nonverbally, expressing resentment through defiant looks, resistant body language, and negative tones of voice. Their attentiveness increases when they are not distracted by the negative feelings from others.

Coaches or instructors can help them refine their technique if they offer help in a positive way when asked, but they need to be careful that the tactile right- brain person does not perceive any negative tones or they will turn off to them. It is better to wait until the tactile right-brain person asks for advice first before offering it, lest it be taken the wrong way.

Tactile right-brain learners like to work in a peaceful environment or a natural setting. They need to be comfortable while studying and will stretch out on the floor or in a chair, or lie on a couch. They can learn with or without music but it has to be music they like or they will be disturbed. They are not distracted by music when they read or study because they do not focus on words; they get a holistic impression of the music, its message and mood from the tune and the words combined, and pick up positive feelings. Some enjoy music that combines the sounds of nature with pleasant music. Music has a calming, relaxing influence, minimizes sad and negative feelings, lifts their spirits, and increases their reading comprehension and ability to learn.

Working in cooperative teams or with one or two people they enjoy can increase their ability to learn because they thrive on the positive feelings from others. Praise, appreciation, and positive nonverbal expression accelerate their learning.

To increase comprehension of what they read, tactile right-brain learners need to feel the written message nonverbally or identify at a feeling level with the subject or character. They can thumb through a book, open a page, and find whatever information they need without reading all of it. They will often skip over details and lengthy explanations to get to the bottom line. Of course, this tendency is useful for fun reading, but for scoring well on a reading test for the ACT or SAT college entrance exam, college boards or certification exams, or on any test for a course or grade, they must use their tactile-right brain strategies to comprehend *every* word, as critical reading and close reading relies on that ability!

They like books that touch their emotions and become bored if they cannot relate to the emotional interaction between characters. When reading about abstract subjects they may personify and assign feelings to the material to make it come alive and comprehend it.

Books that are rich in imagination and have depth, feeling, or a powerful message appeal to them. They like how-to and self-help books dealing with feelings and relationships. After reading, they comprehend the text if they make sketches, drawings, or iconic symbols as they go along. When note taking, they write key words, preferably in color or with an artistic design. Note taking in a pictorial or diagram form, such as a mind map, helps tactile right-brain learners comprehend them better.

In the workforce, they may be writers, artists, photographers, film makers, dancers, or musicians. They may work in engineering; architecture; city planning; technical writing; designing electronic, technical, or computer equipment; drafting; electrical work; construction; building; farming; gardening; landscaping; floral arranging; painting; plumbing; wallpapering; culinary arts; or any field involving their hands. They can find easier, more efficient, and more creative ways of doing these jobs and will look at them through a perspective that no one had thought of before.

Some may be involved with acting, often looking at life in new ways. If they go into acting they are good at portraying the feelings of other people. Their sensitivity to other people's feelings may involve tactile right-brain learners in professions that allow them to alleviate others people's suffering or help people such as social work, psychology, therapy, education, medicine, health, humanitarian projects, or working for peace.

In whatever field they go into, they will provide the feeling content, the imagination, the nonverbal connection between people, and move the hearts of others.

Adapting Learning to a Tactile Right-Brain Style to Improve Reading Comprehension

Tactile right-brain people should ask instructors to provide the big picture or overview using short, sensory language to help them comprehend. They should be allowed to draw, do hands-on projects, or make a mind map in a global, creative, free-flowing way. Since it is hard for them to follow auditory presentations, when note taking or doing study or test taking skills, tactile right-brain learners need a written copy of the notes or readings complete with illustrations or photographs.

They should convert each word at their own pace into: a) a movie in their mind in which they relate the subject or characters with their own feelings; b) colorful, artistic, and creative drawings; c) mind maps showing the main topic and details and their interconnections; d) hands-on projects; or e) decorative and colorfully written words, calligraphy, or designs. They need to observe real-life demonstrations and draw a mind map that gives the big picture to improve their reading comprehension.

CHAPTER 16:

WHAT IS A KINESTHETIC LEFT-BRAIN LEARNER AND HOW TO IMPROVE READING COMPREHENSION QUICKLY?

What Is a Kinesthetic Left-Brain Learner?

Kinesthetic left-brain learners comprehend and learn quickly and can improve reading comprehension and memory through movement and action of their body and large motor muscles in an organized, systematic way.

Because the language function is in the left side of the brain, they can verbalize movement activities in systematic, structured ways.

Kinesthetic left-brain learners need to move a great deal and are restless when they have to stay in one place. If they are forced to stay in one seat too long, they will begin to move or rock in the seat, kick their legs, or get out of the seat spontaneously. Others sitting nearby may be distracted by their movements. Yet if they are given an opportunity to use their body, kinesthetic left- brain learners will actually stick to a task with great concentration; it is when they are denied movement that they find some other outlet for their kinesthetic needs that may not be productive. They are going to move anyway, whether they are restricted or not—so at least their lessons should be structured in a way that includes movement as a positive part of their training.

They like team sports, organized games, or exercises that have rules and are done in a step-by-step way. Many kinesthetic left-brain people are extremely coordinated and can time their movements to be in synch with others. They may excel in synchronous swimming, gymnastics, acrobatics, or choreographed dance.

Not all kinesthetic left-brain people are athletic and coordinated, but they still require sequential movement activities in other fields, whether they are developing real estate, designing a software program or app, find a cure for a disease, or exploring a new hobby. Movement for them can be just mentally moving from one topic or project to another. They are systematic and orderly and tend to stick to and complete a task before moving on.

They need room to move around and comfortable sitting areas to stretch out and relax. If a place does not allow them to move about or has no action-oriented activity, kinesthetic left-brain people will feel uncomfortable and bored because there is nothing for them to do there.

They enjoy talking with other people while in motion or physically doing something, such as jogging, exercising, or working with someone else.

How Kinesthetic Left-Brain Learners Can Improve Reading Comprehension to Learn Anything Quickly

Kinesthetic left-brain learners can improve their reaching comprehension to learn quickly by using an organized, systematic, step-by-step approach that involves moving their bodies and muscles. They are language-oriented, so they can describe what they are doing and follow verbal systematic directions for movement activities. They can get on an exercise bike and read or study while pedaling, or walk around the room while memorizing the lines to a play. Learning games, simulations, role-playing and competitions are great ways for them to learn. Whatever movement they do, they prefer to use a formula, structure, or outline for their work.

It may appear to others that kinesthetic left-brain people are not listening because they are constantly moving, and they process thought better when their eyes are down and away from a speaker, but they are attentive when they are in motion. It is so stressful for them to sit still with their eyes on a speaker that they cannot concentrate on listening. Yet when they are moving about, they are relaxed, comfortable, and attentive.

Hands-on materials and manipulatives are important to kinesthetic learners, but they benefit more and comprehend better from moving their entire bodies, not just their hands. The simple act of standing up helps them comprehend and learn because it gets their legs, arms, and other muscles moving. To comprehend better, they need to write with large markers or chalk on a flip chart, white board, or chalkboard while standing. Doing math problems or outlining a report on a flip chart helps them to think and comprehend better. By writing in large letters on a whiteboard, they can involve their arm muscles and the activity into the kinesthetic realm.

Kinesthetic left-brain people do not prefer to doodle or draw as tactile learners do, but they may do so only when it is the only movement they are permitted in a constrained work or learning situation. It offers them some movement of their arm and hands, which may not fully satisfy them but it is better than sitting still.

In whatever subject they learn, kinesthetic left- brain learners need to comprehend by doing something in a sequential way. Just listening to lectures and verbal explanations is not enough for them to assimilate and comprehend the material. They can benefit by volunteering to be a how-to demonstrator instead of just watching a demonstration. If they hear action words in sequential order, they will physically understand the material. They need a coach who will actively work through the steps of a process. If they are learning how to use a computer, they have to be at a computer while going through each step. If they are learning about carpentry, they will need the tools and materials so as the instructor models for them how to build something they can do it as they learn. They will comprehend not what an instructor does, but what *they* do.

When doing study skills or note taking to learn material for a test or examination, they recall what they did with the material. For study skills, kinesthetic left- brain learners need to act out or dramatize the material, either physically or in their mind, so they can remember what their body did or what they imagined doing. If the subject is math or science, they need to work out the problems or experiments in a step-by-step way in real- life applications, for example, by doing the math required for sending a spaceship to the moon, mixing chemicals to produce medicine, or writing a software program. If circumstances do not allow a kinesthetic left-brain learner to do an activity, their next best resort is to watch the activity—movies on television or in a theater, using streaming video, or watching a program on the Internet or on any electronic device, preferably sequentially-presented programs.

Another kinesthetic method for them is to visualize themselves moving in their mind. In this way they can experience the action within themselves without being noticeable to others. They should feel in their mind that their body is moving or enacting whatever it is they are trying to learn, even while their physical body remains still. This will also activate neuronal growth in their brain as if they had actually physically performed the action.

Kinesthetic left-brain learners thrive on achievement, winning, challenges, and discovery. Being goal-oriented, they enjoy the thrill of the game, and their motivation increases in a competitive environment. They like competing with themselves and beating their own record or playing against teams. Since the left side of the brain handles facts and figures, kinesthetic left-brainers tend to discuss game scores or keep records of achievement of others or themselves. Converting any learning experience into a competitive game helps kinesthetic left-brain people learn better.

Kinesthetic left-brain learners need manipulatives; organized games; building materials; sports equipment, such as balls, basketball hoops, jump ropes, and exercise bikes; science projects; large markers to write on large pieces of paper, flip charts, or white boards; computers; musical instruments; hands-on models; kits; or real objects to move. They like high action yet structured programs, games, and apps on the computer or any electronic digital device.

Kinesthetic left-brain learners can read, work, or study with or without music. Moving or dancing to the rhythm and beat of music can stimulate them to work better. When their muscles are in motion, stress is reduced, their attention and motivation increase, and they learn faster. Kinesthetic left-brain people enjoy playing musical instruments that engage the whole body. They can handle a systematic approach to learning an instrument and will attend to the technical aspects of playing, such as timing, rhythm, and reading music.

Working in cooperative groups or teams helps the kinesthetic left-brain learner because they can move around from group to group. They like to work from a plan or structured outline, so they know each step of the process beforehand. Interaction with different people in different groups fulfills their need to be where the action is.

To improve reading comprehension to learn anything quickly, kinesthetic left-brain learners should get actively involved in the reading material, either by physically acting out the text or imaging themselves doing so. They should imagine experiencing their muscles moving by acting out in their mind what the words describe in sequential order. To engage their interest and comprehend what they read, kinesthetic left- brain learners need to convert the words into an action movie in their mind in which they are part of the action. They tend to forget whatever they do not imagine themselves doing in their mind as they read.

Kinesthetic left-brain learners prefer to read action-packed books. They like to read about movement- oriented activities in a detailed, step-by-step, well- organized way if it can help them improve what they do. The left brain's ability to think in terms of language helps them understand verbal or written directions for action-oriented subjects. They enjoy how-to books that help them perform better if written in logical, sequential ways. Business people enjoy reading how-to suggestions for improving their businesses. Sports lovers enjoy books that help them perfect their techniques.

Kinesthetic left-brain learners need a purpose and action-oriented reason to be motivated to read. If they know their sales will increase if they read the training manual, they will be sure to read it. If they know they need to pass the driver's license examination, they will force themselves to read the manual.

In the work place, kinesthetic left-brain people can be found in jobs that require movement along with left-brain organization, putting what they do into words, or giving detailed verbal directions to others. Jobs that require traveling, speaking, and being clear and organized in one's presentation are found in sales, marketing, district management, owning a self-employed business, teaching, and training. Kinesthetic left-brain people who go into the sciences may be involved in experiments, research and laboratory work, or medical fields, becoming doctors and nurses.

Since they excel at movement jobs that are related to being on time, a function of the left side of the brain, they may be pilots, train conductors, chauffeurs, truck drivers, delivery people, or parcel, express mail, or postal workers. Work that involves the physical body and using details, measurements, and precision are construction, engineering, roadwork, farming, painting, wallpapering, plumbing, electrical work, cleaning, furniture crafting, and doing repair work. Jobs that require physically protecting other people and that use the left-brain attention to structure, organization, and rules are in areas such as the armed forces, such as in the Army, the Navy, the Coast Guard or the Marines, or in the police force, fire department, or secret service.

Kinesthetic left-brain learners may be involved in organized sports and games or may use their verbal abilities to become sportscasters or coaches and instructors in movement fields such as aerobics, exercise, or dance. They may write action stories, sports columns, reviews of movies, dance, or theatrical performances, or organized and structured how-to books. Their ability to visualize action on a screen or stage may make them good screenwriters and playwrights. As artists, they are structured and systematic in their work and will portray detailed action through illustrations, cartoons, comic strips, or commercials for advertising. They may be directors of movies, plays, or dance groups. They may become actors and actresses, musicians, performers, or instructors of performing arts that require body movement.

Adapting Learning to a Kinesthetic Left-Brain Style to Improve Reading Comprehension

Kinesthetic left-brain learners should ask instructors to let them do movement activities in a sequential way to help them comprehend the material. If instruction is presented as a lecture, they need to ask for outlines or study guides or do their own note taking in sequential order, so they can convert the words into: a) actions; b) a movie in their mind in which they imagine themselves doing the action; or c) an outline while they stand up and write it in large size on a flip chart or white board. They can find sequential material, either written and in audio- visual format that relates to the subject and convert the text into a physical action or an imagined action in their mind.

CHAPTER 17:

WHAT IS A KINESTHETIC RIGHT-BRAIN LEARNER AND HOW TO IMPROVE READING COMPREHENSION QUICKLY?

What Is A Kinesthetic Right-Brain Learner?

Kinesthetic right-brain learners can improve reading comprehension to learn quickly through moving their gross motor muscles in a creative, imaginative, free- flowing, and unstructured way. They do not think or comprehend in words, but get information intuitively.

They become highly restless if forced to stay still or remain in one place too long. Kinesthetic right-brain learners will feel so constrained and physically stressed that they will start to move around anyway. Their need to keep moving and changing activities may make they look hyperactive to others. It is actually when they are denied movement that they look distracted. It is better to give them movement activities related to the learning task, such as learning games, exercises, or simulations.

They will then be able to concentrate as well as people of other styles do when working in their element. Unless given productive activities related to their work, they will kick or swing their legs under the table, drum on the tabletop, slouch, rock in their seats, or find excuses to get up, whether it is to get a snack or look out a window.

Not all kinesthetic right-brain learners are athletes. There are many other activities that involve movement. For them, movement can be moving in their mind from one topic or project to another.

Kinesthetic right-brain learners can think about several things simultaneously and can have many projects going on at once. They can keep each one straight in their minds without any difficulty. They work in an impulsive, quick way, wanting to see results immediately so they can move on to another activity. In the rush to complete a project, they may not worry about whether the parts were done to perfection. They see the whole picture, not the details.

There are times when they consider a job done just by having thought of it. Some kinesthetic right-brain people put the idea out, do some preliminary work, and move on to another project. It is up to the detail-oriented people around them to pick up the pieces and complete the task so they can then move on to create new inventions. They have a wealth of new ideas and discoveries, like a brainstorm session in motion, giving the world a seeming endless supply of novel, unique ideas.

Being goal-oriented, kinesthetic right-brain learners have the ability to get things done, handling many projects at once. They are not time-oriented, so they do not tend to stick to schedules, routines, or time constraints. They are go-with-the-flow people who will do what they feel like at the moment. They can keep work moving and be a wealth of creativity and imagination, although others have to be willing to accept their lack of consciousness of time. At work, as frequently as they arrive late, they may also become so absorbed in a task that they may stay overtime just to complete it, giving you more productivity than what you are paying them to do!

A kinesthetic right-brain learner needs a comfortable

environment, full of activity, with room to stretch out and move. Some will get up and leave if they are bored or in a restricted environment. Being outdoors is high on their list because there they can move freely.

Kinesthetic right-brain people enjoy being with other people when they can do something together that does not require a lot of talk. Watch them during a football game and you may hear grunts, moans, or cheers. They can communicate action without speaking and use their body and arms to dramatize or express what they want to describe. When they do talk, they use short action words and get to the point quickly.

How Kinesthetic Right-Brain Learners Can Improve Reading Comprehension to Learn Anything Quickly

Kinesthetic right-brain people can improve reading comprehension to learn quickly by moving in an unstructured, imaginative, and free-flowing way. They need to use their bodies and muscles to learn. Thus, they can comprehend better while cycling on a stationary bike, memorizing material by jumping rope, simulating or role-playing a situation, performing experiments, or playing creative games.

Kinesthetic right-brain learners, often adventuresome and daring, enjoy challenges. This group just needs to jump in and do it. They pick up the how- to information by intuition or gut feelings and learn by trial and error, exploration, and discovery. They fully grasp the overall patterns of any situation and know what to do. Their excellent visual-spatial relations, intuition, and quick reflexes enable them to look at a problem, instantaneously judge a situation, and move accordingly, without words or written directions, to find the solution.

Kinesthetic right-brain learners do not require step-by-step, detailed instructions. They are whole-to- part learners who need to see the big picture or overview first and fill in the details later. For example, they will not give a detailed verbal account of a sports event—they will give the highlights and the winning score: the bottom line. If they see an entire math problem worked out with the answer and several examples, they can figure out how to solve similar problems.

Kinesthetic right-brain learners listen better to others while in motion, with their eyes focused down and away from the speaker. They comprehend more when they are in motion than when they are sitting still. When they are moving, they can relax, concentrate, and absorb information better.

They learn and comprehend better by standing up to work. Writing on a flip chart or whiteboard with large markers works better for them than writing while sitting.

By involving their whole arm, legs, and body, they can put the activity into the kinesthetic realm. Making a mind map of material they need to know by using their whole arm to write provides more activity and helps them comprehend what they learned. They doodle not because of a tactile need to write but because it offers more movement than sitting still.

They need active real-life or simulated experiences. For example, when learning about accounting, they would prepare a budget for a real company or an imaginary one they created for this learning experience. If volunteers are needed for a demonstration, kinesthetic right-brain learners jump at a chance to get out of their seats and do something. If they are learning a dance, they will comprehend it not by watching someone else do it, but by doing it themselves. They need to immerse themselves fully in the experience in an unstructured way. Many of them do not want long explanations; they want to figure something out for themselves. They need teachers who will take on the role of a coach, use only key action words, and guide them if they ask for help.

If a situation does not permit the kinesthetic right-brain learner to do an activity, their next resort is to watch activity on television, DVDs, videos, or movies.

To comprehend what they learn, they need to act out the material or visualize themselves dramatizing it as if a movie were playing in their head. When they visualize they need to feel the movement in their muscles. Their body may move and sway as they go through the movements in their mind. When they receive directions to drive to a friend's house, they experience themselves turning the car right or left, or whipping along the curve in the road in their mind.

Good learning materials for a kinesthetic right- brain learner are manipulatives, games, building materials, tools, sports equipment, balls, exercise bikes, large flip charts and whiteboards, large markers, computers with action games, percussion instruments, guitars or organs, rhythmic music, hands-on models, or real objects to move. They like unstructured, nonsequential, high-action, fast-moving video games, apps, and interactive programs. If a computer program is too slow or too structured, they become bored. They prefer moving a mouse, joystick, or swiping their fingers across a screen rather than using keystrokes on a keyboard.

Competitions and challenges interest kinesthetic right-brain people, either in games or on the job. They may participate in contests that determine who can sell or produce the most. They are goal-oriented and enjoy the thrill of winning points for themselves or their team.

Make a game of anything and they will learn it Kinesthetic right-brain learners do better using note taking, study skills and test taking strategies by remembering what action they *did* while learning. For them to concentrate, distractions caused by the movement of others have to be eliminated. Working in a study carrel, using a divider, or facing a wall can keep them from noticing the movement of others, but they have to be comfortable while studying. Being stretched out on the floor or couch gives their muscles freedom of movement. They can work and study with or without music. Because they do not listen to the words, music does not interfere with their reading. The rhythm or beat stimulates their muscles to move or dance in time to the music. Their stress is reduced and their attention and motivation increases.

By working in cooperative groups, kinesthetic right-brain learners have an opportunity to move around more from group to group. They thrive on change and on interacting with different people to satisfy their need for action.

To improve memory and reading comprehension, kinesthetic right-brain learners need to convert words into a movie in which they are part of the action.

Imagining that they are the director of a movie and converting the book or script into action scenes, while describing the action that would appear on their movie screen, will make a book come alive for them. Whatever they do not feel themselves doing—or imagining they are doing—as they read will not be comprehended.

They read for the main idea or big picture, skipping small details, and are impatient with too many words. Thus, they tend to miss reading comprehension questions that deal with details, time sequence, or abstract ideas. It is not that they cannot comprehend the details, but they need kinesthetic right-brain techniques to master them.

Kinesthetic right-brain learners prefer short or highly action-packed books or how-to books that help them perform better. Unlike their left-brain counterparts, they need diagrams, photographs, or illustrations. They do not like to read a book from cover to cover but tend to skip around, getting what they need from it. They may learn by just looking at the pictures, glancing at the captions, or flipping through the pages, catching stray sentences that may give them all they need to know about a topic. They have an intuitive sense that helps them find what they need.

Kinesthetic right-brain learners need to know the end product before they start. Thus, they need to know the reason they are reading something. They will be motivated if they feel it will help them do something better. Watch them zip through a book if they feel it will help them be the top in their field, boost their sales, or get a promotion. Books with summaries or key points at the beginning or end of the chapter help them find what is important and relevant to them.

In the workforce, kinesthetic right-brain people can be found in jobs that require movement and frequent change. They may not attend to details, but they will work quickly to get a job done rapidly. With this group, speed and completion takes priority over spending a great deal of time on detail, as long as the end product works.

As scientists, kinesthetic right-brain people enjoy

inventing, doing research and laboratory work, or experimenting in the fields of paleontology, anthropology, quantum physics, or chemistry. If they go into medicine, they may run their own practices so they can have the freedom to set their own hours, or move from one patient to another in ten different rooms.

They may be involved in sports fields, as athletes, coaches, instructors, trainers, or owning a sports facility or team. They may be involved with dancing, gymnastics, golf, track, skiing, skating, swimming, sailing, snorkeling, surfing, biking, gymnastics, horseback riding, Rollerblading, karate, judo, horseback riding, or aerobics, and so on. They may play football, soccer, hockey, tennis, and basketball for fun, but may have to work harder to adjusting to being on an organized professional team because of the rigors of the schedule, discipline, and routine involved in that lifestyle.

They may enjoy the adventure and risks involved in police work, firefighting, the space program, or the Army, Navy, Marines, or Coast Guard. Many of them like to be self-employed so they do not have to follow someone else's schedule. They may run their own computer, construction, painting, wallpapering, moving, lawn, maintenance, plumbing, electrical, or repair companies.

They can be involved in building, making, or fixing things such as cars, houses, boats, motorcycles, computers, appliances, machines, or furniture. They may do work that requires physical exertion such as construction, building bridges, or lifting boxes. Some work in jobs that require traveling, but with little talk.

Long-distance driving, flying, chauffeuring, making deliveries, and trucking may satisfy their need to move, if they are not constrained by time schedules.

Kinesthetic right-brain writers write short action stories that get to the point or how-to books that give key points without much detail. If they are artists, they like art requiring action—huge canvasses or sculptures with strong movement of color and design. They tend to make quick, impressionistic drawings that give a general idea of what they are trying to say. If they are actors or actresses, they may prefer parts with less talk and more action or be stunt people. If they are musicians, they enjoy playing instruments in which they can move their body. If they are singers, they prefer doing so with movement or dance. Kinesthetic right-brain learners tend to be better at playing by ear rather than reading notes.

They also tend to be imaginative and can come up with new tunes or forms of music.

Their imagination, new ideas, openness to change, and inventiveness make them an excellent resource. Their commitment to doing makes them product oriented and able to produce a large amount of work in a short amount of time. As they move, the world also moves forward into new avenues and directions.

Adapting Learning to a Kinesthetic Right-Brain Style to Improve Reading Comprehension

Kinesthetic right-brain learners need to ask instructor to provide the big picture or overview using short, sensory language and let them do kinesthetic activities in a global, creative, free-flowing way to help them comprehend better. Since it is hard for kinesthetic right- brain learners to follow auditory presentations, they need a written copy of the notes or readings or take dictation of a lecture and convert each word into: a) a movie in their mind in which they imagine and feel themselves acting out the parts; b) a drawing they make with key words or numbers in colorful, artistic, and creative ways, while standing up at a white board or flip chart and writing with their large arm muscles; c) a mind map in color in which they show the main topic, the details, and their interconnections; or d) a kinesthetic project. They may need to find corresponding pictures, movies, or activities, in which they can participate in real-life demonstrations. They can convert information into a mind map that gives the big picture of the subject they are learning.

PART 5:

ACCELERATED LEARNING: HOW TO IMPROVE READING COMPREHENSION USING YOUR SUPERLINK LEARNING STYLE AND BRAIN STYLE

CHAPTER 18:

AN EASY 7-STEP PLAN FOR IMPROVING READING COMPREHENSION TO LEARN ANYTHING QUICKLY

When you discover your best superlink reading comprehension and learning style and brain style, you are ready for this easy7-step plan to apply this knowledge to comprehend anything quickly. You will be able to improve your reading comprehension through your brain's fastest superlink reading comprehension and learning style and brain style. You will discover the ingredients for comprehending anything using your best superlink. The seven-step formula to rapid learning is:

Step 1: Know Your Brain Fastest Superlink to Reading Comprehension: In the earlier part of the book, you discovered your brain's own unique fastest and best way of comprehending to apply to any subject.

Step 2: Preparation and Planning: Next, you will plan your own program, beginning with the prelearning activities that will put you in the right frame of mind to comprehend quickly.

Step 3: Input: Then, you will find out what type of instruction, learning materials, and learning environment is needed to improve your reading comprehension.

Step 4: Reading and Listening Comprehension: Next, you will find out how to increase your comprehension of what you read and hear to improve reading and listening comprehension.

Step 5: Improve Your Reading Comprehension: Then, you will learn how to improve your reading comprehension and retention to optimize learning.

Step 6: Note-taking, Study Skills, and Test-taking Skills: You will also learn how you can retain what you learned in your long term-memory by sharpening your note taking, test-taking skills, and study skills to improve your performance.

Step 7: Application: Finally, you will learn how to apply what you comprehend to your current situation.

The following section of the book is set up so that you can pick a subject you want to comprehend and use this guide to help you understand the subject quickly.

Depending on your superlinks reading comprehension and learning style and brain style, you can read silently or aloud, take notes, or do the activities suggested for each chapter with a subject you want to comprehend so that you will be doing the book, instead of just passively reading it.

Select a subject you want to comprehend right away. The subject can be a course you are currently taking or a self-study program. It could be a topic you wish to learn about on your own or one that you will need to pass a test or qualifying exam, such as a GRE, SAT, ACT, etc., or bar or medical examination. It can be a skill you want to comprehend, such as learning a computer software program, building a deck, or playing golf. Many of the activities in this book lend themselves well to courses that require reading a textbook or listening to oral presentations, but the process can be applied equally well to learning a vocation, craft, sport, hobby, or a skill required on your job. Even in a performance task you need to receive information from reading, listening, taking notes, doing something with your hands, or engaging your body. You will discover which reading comprehension method is the best for you no matter what area you wish to learn.

Thus, as you continue through this book, you will be learning two things:

1) how to comprehend anything quickly, and
2) the *subject* that you want to comprehend quickly. Once you master these techniques, you can use them for any subject or field you wish to understand throughout the rest of your life.

Exercise: Select the subject, topic, or skill you want to comprehend.

CHAPTER 19:
PREPARATION AND PLANNING FOR IMPROVING READING COMPREHENSION QUICKLY

You are now ready to begin the process of improving your reading comprehension. The first steps are to ask yourself the following questions before you get started:

- What is my motivation, purpose, or goal for wanting to comprehend this subject?
- What do I already comprehend about this subject? What else do I need to comprehend about this subject?
- What is the best way for me to comprehend what I learn?
- How can I raise my self-esteem and use positive thinking about myself?
- What are some relaxation and stress reduction techniques to optimize my reading comprehension? How can I visualize success?

What Is My Motivation, Purpose, or Goal for Wanting to Comprehend This Subject?

People comprehend things that serve a purpose in their lives. Every day we are bombarded with information that we see, hear, smell, taste, or touch, but we only comprehend what we consider important; otherwise, we would be unable to sort through the multitude of stimuli we receive.

Our brain has the decision-making capacity to sort out what is relevant. Whatever it decides to comprehend, it will comprehend. This is a choice we make continually and it is something we should keep in mind when it comes to learning. As information is conveyed to us, we can observe it passively and let it bounce off us, or we can take it in and retain it. Think about several subjects you have learned throughout your life. Were there times when you attended a lecture or read a book, hearing and seeing the words, but moments later the information was gone? You did not really *learn* the material—you did not fully comprehend it. Were there other times when you decided that you really needed to comprehend the information you received so you paid close attention to it, absorbed it, and comprehended it? Somehow, you made a decision to comprehend it because you had an important reason for doing so, whether you wanted to excel at your job or you had an important test to pass. Whatever the reason, your learning increased because you had the motivation or a purpose for learning it.

Motivation to learn and comprehend is a key ingredient in presetting your mind for comprehension. If you take a few seconds at the start of any learning session and say, What is my purpose or goal for comprehending this material? you will have programmed your mind to be attentive and interested. The more relevant the subject is to your life, the greater the chance you have for keeping your attention fully on the subject to comprehend it.

Determine why you need to comprehend the subject you selected and keep this goal in mind as you learn the new material.

Exercise: Write down your reason for wanting to comprehend the subject.

What Do I Already Comprehend About the Subject?

The next step in the planning stage of your learning is to evaluate what you already know and comprehend about the subject. To accelerate your learning you will need to fit the instruction into the shortest possible time. One way to do that is to eliminate wasting time relearning what you already know. Time and life are too short to sit through the same material repeatedly. You want to focus on new information.

To make this evaluation, list what you already comprehend about the subject. Only write down what you are sure that you comprehend because you may need a refresher for some material. As you go through your learning program, you can skip or skim over what you already comprehend to save time.

Exercise: Write down what you already comprehend about the subject:

What Else Do I Need to Comprehend About This Subject?

After determining what you already comprehend, the next step is to evaluate what else you *need* to comprehend about the subject. Most people go blindly into a subject. They plod along from one point to the next, starting at the front cover of a book and ending at the back. If the book contains topics not relevant, you should skip them to avoid being slowed down.

If you take a course, then you will probably be guided by

an instructor who will tell you what you need to comprehend. If you are doing a self-study program, you need to do some preparation in advance and find out what you want to comprehend about the subject. Do you want to master a certain process or skill and cover certain topics? Do you want to show proficiency in one area or know everything that was ever written about that subject? Decide what it is you need to comprehend to satisfy your goals. List those topics and use that list as your guide. In this way, you can select the most helpful material and skip what is irrelevant to your learning plan.

Exercise: Write down what else you need to comprehend about the subject.

What Is My Best Way to Comprehend?

Discovering your superlink reading comprehension and learning style and brain style is an important ingredient in the entire learning process. Using reading comprehension methods that are compatible with your superlink can be a key factor in determining how successfully and quickly you will comprehend the subject. By matching the right methods and materials to how your brain comprehends, you accelerate learning by eliminating unnecessary barriers that can slow down learning.

Exercise: Review the information on your superlink reading comprehension and learning style and brain style described in this book and list the best reading comprehension methods and materials for you to learn.

How Can I Use Positive Thinking to Comprehend Anything Quickly and Raise My Confidence and Self- esteem?

If you had a hard time learning in school, you may not have enough confidence in yourself and your abilities. Perhaps you saw others earn high grades while you received low grades or even failed. This may have resulted in low self-esteem, negative thoughts about yourself, or thinking there is something wrong with you. Unfortunately, years of this kind of negative attitude may become a self-fulfilling prophecy. When we think we can't do something, we put so much energy into that negative thought that we may end up not succeeding. On the other hand, when we think we can succeed, we work with confidence and end up succeeding.

One study conducted by Harvard researchers, led by Robert Rosenthal, and that later became known as Pygmalion in the Classroom, focused on a group of ninety students of average ability. Three teachers to whom they were assigned in classes of thirty each were told that they were gifted students. The teachers, thinking that they had gifted students, taught them as if they *were* gifted and had high expectations of them. At the end of the study, the progress of each group was measured. The results were that the students met those expectations, did exceedingly well, and their achievement soared. (Canter, Lee, and Canter, Marlene. *The High Performing Teacher; Avoiding Burnout and Increasing Your Motivation*: A Publication of Lee Canter and Associates, Santa Monica, CA. 1994, pp. 25-26). What this study points out is that our performance can be influenced by our expectations of ourselves as well as others' expectations of us.

You might have been slowed down because you were not

taught in your best reading comprehension and learning style and brain style. You learned quickly in the first few years of life because you were allowed to use your natural way of learning—the learning method that is easiest for you—which may have been any of the following: watching, listening, exploring, playing learning games, hands-on learning, or any other method. But in traditional schools students are usually taught in one or two ways, mostly by watching (a visual method) or listening to the teacher (an auditory one). If students do not have the same reading comprehension and learning style as the one used in the classroom they struggle to learn. During the time they spend trying to adapt to a reading comprehension and learning style that is not compatible with their own, the class has already moved on. These students do not know what is wrong with them or why others are getting it and they are not. They do not know that if they were taught in a reading comprehension and learning style and brain style that matched their own they would move along as quickly as some of the other students. But the students do not know what to ask for. They are prisoners of a system that is not working for them.

If you are one of those who experienced failure or felt you could not learn and comprehend as quickly as others, or were a good student and wanted to be better and could not, you were probably just as bright as those other children, but were limited by a learning and reading comprehension method that was not compatible with your own. The students who did well may have been those whose superlink reading comprehension style matched the teacher's presentation. If you were to take those who did well and put them in a learning environment that is not compatible with their reading comprehension and learning style, they also might struggle or find it harder to achieve.

How can we raise our self-esteem? First, realize that *every* human being has an amazing capacity to learn and comprehend. In the first seven years of life, children can memorize an entire language and the meaning of thousands of words. Our brain's ability to comprehend does not shut down after first grade. There is nothing inherent in any of us that says that we suddenly become incapable of learning and comprehending when we arrive at the doors of an elementary school. The same brain and ability to comprehend that you used to assimilate an entire language in the first seven years of life is just as intelligent and prepared to learn after it begins school. To raise your self-esteem, realize that what happened to you in the past may not have been your fault. Had you been taught in your best reading comprehension and learning style and brain style you would have learned and comprehended faster and more easily. What is past is past and now you know how *you* need to comprehend.

Start from today. Feel confident that you now have a reading comprehension approach that will work for you. As you begin to learn through the approach that matches your superlink reading comprehension and learning style and brain style, you will experience the feeling that others who have done so have experienced—you *can* do it. It is easy, fun, and natural. Having positive learning experiences will help you to start feeling good about yourself. Slowly, those feelings of past failures will fade.

You need to start a cycle of success. How is this done? Firstly, think of a time in which you succeeded at a task. It could have been a school subject, an extracurricular activity, or something you did on your own at home. Try to relive the experience in your mind. How did it feel to succeed? Did you feel happy, proud, and confident? Did you want to repeat the experience? Most people would say they would like to repeat the task because of the good feelings that accompanied the experience.

Now think of a time when you failed at something. It could have been a school subject, a sport or hobby, or something you did at home. How did you feel? Did you feel hurt, angry, frustrated, stupid, or hopeless? Did you want to repeat that task again? Most people, unless they wanted to repeat it just to prove to themselves they could do it, would say they did not want to repeat the task. Thus, because of the pain of the experience, they began to avoid the very area in which they may have needed to practice. The more they avoided practicing, the further they grew from mastering it. The cycle of failure began. The initial failure caused them to avoid the task, get further behind, and reinforced more failure.

It is time to break the cycle. By learning according to your best superlink reading comprehension and learning style and brain style, you will now find it easier to comprehend. Gain confidence. Start with some easy work to regain the good feelings that come with success. Then, as you find you can finally succeed, slowly add harder and more challenging material. Do not frustrate yourself by beginning with comprehending material that is too hard. Until you regain your self- esteem, master the technique of comprehending in your best superlink reading comprehension and learning style using some review material. Then add new material as you regain confidence.

Whatever your level of education, know that you carry in

your head a most remarkable computer. You just have to fit compatible software into the hardware of your brain for it to run properly. Many others who have tried these reading comprehension methods have succeeded, and you can, too!

Exercise: Tell yourself, I can raise my self-esteem and positive thoughts about myself by realizing the possible causes of my previous struggles with learning and reading comprehension. List subjects with which you previously had trouble, analyze how they were taught and how the methods may not have been compatible with your best reading comprehension and learning style. List methods from earlier parts of this book compatible with your superlink reading comprehension and learning style and brain style that could have been used to make those subjects easier to comprehend.

Why Are Relaxation and Stress Reduction Techniques Important to Optimize Reading Comprehension?

Relaxation and stress reduction can improve reading comprehension. Medical research over the past decades has been exploring the connection between the mind and body. When we are in a state of fear or extreme stress, the body's survival reaction is to shut down our higher- level thinking portion and respond according to the part of the brain that deals with the fight or flight response.

We respond with physiological reactions such as increases of adrenaline, rapid heartbeats, and constricted blood vessels. Your body is readying itself to run or fight, requiring the use of your arms and legs. During this state, you are not ready to comprehend a mathematical theorem or new vocabulary words.

People who had negative experiences of failure in the classroom enter into this state of panic and fear when it comes to learning. Test taking may cause them to be fearful so they do not score well even if they studied.

Their teachers or parents may have been upset with them, inflicted physical, psychological, or emotional pain and punishment, called them demeaning names, or ostracized them because of their mistakes at school.

Years of reliving this trauma may cause people to enter a state of stress, panic, and fear when they have to comprehend something new. For successful learning to take place we need to learn how to relax and reduce stress. We have to program ourselves to break the cycle of failure and get out of the habit of fearing learning.

Relaxation and stress-reduction techniques can assist in the process by improving reading comprehension.

Step one is to put the past behind you and realize that these struggles with reading comprehension or test taking may not have been entirely your fault, and remind yourself that the fear response is only a habit. You now know what you need in order to comprehend; things *will* be different this time. By following a new approach that suits your reading comprehension style, you will be more successful. So relax—this time you *will* succeed!

Step two is to get your body into a physiological state of relaxation. Our brain waves run at different frequencies. From thirteen to twenty Hz (Hertz) or cps (cycles per second) we are in the beta state, the state in which we function at work, driving, or in the fight–or–flight mode. From nine to twelve Hz we are in the alpha state, in which we are more relaxed, but alert. The alpha state is good for learning. The theta state, from five to eight Hz, is the meditation state. That is good for relaxation and stress reduction. From one to four Hz we are in the delta state, which is deep sleep. Before trying to comprehend material for the subject we are learning, we may want to reduce our stress and increase our relaxation by entering into the theta state—the state of meditation. There are different ways to do this.

One way to reach the state of relaxation is to slow down our breathing. In fear, the hormones we release increase our heart rate. To reduce a rapid heart rate and to relax, find a place to sit in a relaxed position. Take some deep breaths, letting the air fill your lungs. Breathe to the count of four, hold for four, and release your breath in four. Do this slow breathing for several minutes, until you feel your heartbeat slow down. As you breathe in, feel relaxation enter you, filling your entire body. Imagine being filled with this relaxation. Feel your stress evaporate as calm and peace fill you. Imagine that relaxation opens you up to receive the wisdom and knowledge to help you learn and comprehend anything you want to know. You can then feel the stress of your body disappear and relaxation fill you.

Another way to get to the theta state is to still your mind and eliminate all thoughts of panic, worry, and fear. Sitting for a few minutes in meditation calms your mind. You can close your eyes in a relaxed manner. Concentrate as if you were watching a movie screen within. Sit in a relaxed manner, looking into the center of what is in front of you. Do not think about anything; just look into the middle of the field of vision. Your mind will become concentrated and focused. A feeling of relaxation will come over your body and mind. By keeping your attention on one point, you will find your powers of concentration become focused and sharp. You may feel a sense of peace. Some people even experience blissful joy. Your worries and fears melt away—you are now in the state where you are ready to comprehend whatever you want.

Some people try a variety of other techniques for relaxation. Some use music to get into this state. Early work with accelerated learning developed by the Bulgarian researcher Georgi Lozanov relied on music to get the mind ready for learning. Baroque music, which contains sixty beats per minute, supposedly synchronizes with the heartbeat, helping people get into an optimal learning state. Musician Steven Halpern has found that music with less than sixty beats per minute also works.

His research reveals that music with a slower beat slows the heart rate, putting the body and mind into a more relaxed state, ideal for learning. He has been a pioneer in producing music to accelerate learning. Some schools have used his music to create a calm, peaceful state in which students can learn with a stress-free attitude.

Some people like to do physical exercise or yoga to get the body relaxed. Exercise or physical yogas stimulates the flow of oxygen through the bloodstream, carrying it to the brain to eliminate mental stress and get the brain ready for learning and comprehending. New research reveals that exercise stimulates the brain to make more connections that can increase learning and improve reading comprehension.

Whatever method you use, the end result is to calm the body and mind to keep them out of the fight-or- flight mode. Before beginning a reading comprehension session, spend five or ten minutes in any of the relaxation techniques. You can do the same one every day, or you can vary them. Find those that work the best for you. The goal is to keep the higher-thinking functions in the brain open so that comprehending the subject you want to learn can take place.

Exercise: Try different stress-reduction activities to find those that are best for you.

How Can I Visualize Success?

The last step in the planning stage for improving reading comprehension is to visualize success. New studies have shown that even thinking about doing a task results in neuron connections being made as if they had physically performed the activity. This is a powerful discovery supported by scientific evidence indicating that by mentally going through a task, brain cells are forming connections for that task, accelerating our learning and improving our reading comprehension. Athletes have been using this technique for years. Before a competition, they visualize or imagine themselves winning. The power of positive mental mind-set and pre- setting brain connections for success is used in other fields as well. Medical researchers and doctors have reported cases in which after the visualization of good health, their patients' health improved. Health and wellness centers around the world have been established, devoted to helping people visualize themselves becoming healthy. The same technique has been used for increasing learning, reading and listening comprehension, and memory.

The technique is simple. Sit quietly in a relaxed state. You can get into a meditative state first so that the body and mind are calm and stilled. Select one of the following next steps based on your reading comprehension and learning style.

For Visual Learners: Picture yourself successfully completing the course in whatever subject you are trying to comprehend.

For Auditory Learners: Hear yourself say that you have successfully completed the course.

For Tactile Learners: Feel the joy of success of completing the course.

For Kinesthetic Learners: Experience yourself jumping up and giving a victory punch with your fist into the air and saying, Yes! after successfully completing the course.

Try to make the image of your successful moment as vivid as possible, using all your senses, with your superlink reading comprehension and learning style and brain style as the main modality. Imagine yourself being actively engaged in some action as a result of your successful learning. Live the successful moment as if it really has already happened. Repeat this activity daily. Know that you have already succeeded. Live each day as one more step leading to the success that is already yours. Students have successfully used this technique to win scholarships or admission into schools in which the competition was fierce.

Visualizing your success as well as doing the steps in this accelerated program of how to comprehend quickly to improve reading and listening comprehension, memory, study skills, note taking, and test-taking skills go hand in hand. The visualization of success adds the power of positive thinking to the reading comprehension tools you are learning. You are now ready to comprehend quickly the subject you have chosen to master.

Exercise: Visualize yourself succeeding at quickly comprehending the subject you chose and write a description of what you visualized.

CHAPTER 20:
CHOOSING YOUR BEST INSTRUCTION, MATERIALS, AND LEARNING ENVIRONMENT TO IMPROVE READING COMPREHENSION QUICKLY

After preparing your mind for optimum learning, you are ready to begin taking in the information you need to learn quickly to improve reading comprehension. You will discover:

- how instruction should be delivered to fit your superlink reading comprehension and learning style and brain style
- the learning materials you should use for your unique superlink reading comprehension style
- the learning environment you need for your brain's fastest superlink reading comprehension style
- how to convert information from your weaker superlink reading comprehension and learning style to your best reading comprehension style

You want to choose the type of instruction, learning materials, and learning environment that will allow you to absorb information that matches your superlink reading comprehension and learning style in order to comprehend anything quickly.

If you have control over your learning plan, you can make the above decisions about the type of information yourself. In many cases, though, you will be learning from others, such as through a course, a required manual, or a curriculum prescribed for your training in your field of work. Some of the above decisions may not rest in your hands but are left up to the instructor or the institution preparing your learning program. The people teaching you may not do so in a way that matches your best reading comprehension and learning style and brain style. In that case, you have two options. The first option is to explain to the instructor or coordinator of your studies how you comprehend best and ask him or her to present the material in a way that is compatible with your superlink reading comprehension and learning and brain style. The second option comes into play when the instructor or coordinator does not want to or cannot present the material in your best reading comprehension style. In that case, you need to learn how to convert the type of instruction to your own best reading comprehension and learning style and brain style. This chapter will teach you how to do this. This ability can be a powerful tool that will enable you to comprehend in *any* situation—you won't need to rely on others to determine whether or not you succeed.

Fit the Instruction and Materials to Your Superlink Reading Comprehension and Learning Style and Brain Style

There are many ways to comprehend a subject. The medium of instruction and the materials are the communication methods used to convey the material. Below are some of the different instructional media and materials.

Written material: books, eBooks, digital downloads, PDFs, textbooks, manuals, guidebooks, booklets, pamphlets, reference materials such as encyclopedias, almanacs, dictionaries, thesauruses, magazines, journals, newspaper, microfilm, microfiche, scripts, screenplays, poetry, charts, lists, diagrams, graphs, faxed material, emails, blogs, e-zine articles, Internet postings, websites, etc.

Graphic material: photographs, illustrations, pictures, drawings, maps, atlases, posters, cartoons, diagrams and charts with graphics, digital graphic downloads, graphic eBooks, PDFs, websites with graphics, illustrated aps, etc.

Audio-Visual Material: aps, digital audio downloads, streaming audio over the Internet, audiotapes, CDs, slides, power-point, filmstrips, DVDs, streaming videos, 3-D movies, radio, television, distance learning through teleconferencing, web conferences, web meetings, and webinars, cable television, educational television, and public broadcasting.

From Computers: information from the Internet, streaming video and audio, software programs, aps, virtual reality, webinars, web conferences, teleseminars, social media, e-mail, distance learning via computer, and on-line courses and degrees programs.

Hands-on Activities: writing, typing, drawing, sketching, painting, creating graphics on the computer, sculpture, building, constructing, arts and crafts, using tools, machinery or equipment, role-playing, simulations, learning games, using manipulatives, dramatization, film-making, video production, theater productions, music productions, demonstrations, making discoveries, exploration, performing experiments, sports, exercises, etc.

Real-life Experiences: on-the-job training, fieldwork, trips to museums, learning centers (such as oceanariums, seaquariums, forest preserves, or environmental centers), or engaging in apprenticeships in stores or retail businesses, service industries, construction sites, hospitals, schools, factories, farms, delivery companies, airports, shipyards, railway stations, banks, the stock exchange, supermarkets, auto repair shops, art studios, theater or dance companies, concert halls, etc.), playing on sports teams (football, baseball, basketball, soccer, hockey, golf, etc.), or engage in training programs coordinated between places of employment and schools, etc.

Personal Instructors: direct instruction from teachers, professors, instructors, guides, mentors, life coaches, athletic or sports coaches, facilitators, trainers, skilled craftspeople, employers, managers or supervisors. (The person may instruct through oral presentations or lectures, reading aloud material to the students or requiring students to read it themselves, providing printed graphic material, audio-visual material, and computer technology, setting up hands-on learning activities, or putting the learners into real-life situations in order to learn.)

Combinations of the above: Any of the above teaching methods can be combined.

Based on the description of your superlink that you read in the earlier part of this book, choose the instructional medium and materials from the above lists that corresponds with your superlinks reading comprehension and learning style and brain style. For example, if you are a visual right-brain person, the medium and materials you need would be graphic material, movies, videos, printed material written in a visual right-brain style, or real life experiences.

If you can control your learning, then you can set it up in the way that will help you comprehend quickly. But we do not always have control over the way we are instructed. We may not be in charge of choosing the best medium or learning material, or selecting the learning environment. Is it hopeless? Absolutely not. What you can do is convert any instruction into your own best reading comprehension style. You can still comprehend the subject even if the medium, material, and environment do not suit your reading comprehension style. The following pages show you the instructional media compatible with your reading comprehension style and how to convert medium not in your style into your best superlink reading comprehension modality. Think of it as a translation system to show you what you can do to turn a poor situation into an optimal one.

The following information will enable you to convert a medium of instruction and materials or some aspect of them into the best medium of instruction and materials for your superlink reading comprehension style.

Converting Instruction and Materials into Your Superlink Reading Comprehension and Learning Style and Brain Style to Improve Reading Comprehension

Superlink: Visual Left-Brain Learners:
Media Type:
Written Material: Ideal for visual left-brain learners.

Graphic Material: Label and describe graphic material.

Audio-Visual Material: Use a corresponding study guide or transcript or take notes to review later.

Computers: When graphics are the only displayed media, search for a corresponding online manual to read that explains the graphics, or do your own note taking.

Hands-On Activities: Read the directions for the activity or write your own.

Real-Life Experiences: Refer to a written description of the activity.

Learning from an Instructor: If the presentation is auditory, tactile, or kinesthetic, make your own outline, directions or study guide to read and comprehend later.

Superlink: Visual Right-Brain Learners:
Media Type:
Written Material: Draw pictures or diagrams to accompany the text.

Graphic Material: This is ideal for visual right-brain learners.

Audio-Visual Material: For written text, or audio media without graphics, create your own sketches or graphic materials in color.

Computers: For programs with written text, draw your own illustrations, graphic images, or mind maps to accompany the text.

Hands-On Activities: Make an illustrated instruction booklet for the activity.

Real-Life Experiences: Take notes in color on the experience and illustrate them.

Learning from an Instructor: If the instruction is auditory, tactile, or kinesthetic, take notes by drawing sketches or graphic images of the material in color.

Superlink: Auditory Left-Brain Learners:
Media Type:
Written Material: Read the material aloud and discuss it.

Graphic Material: Talk about the material to yourself aloud or discuss it with others.

Audio-Visual Material: Ideal for auditory left-brain learners. For visual media without sound, talk about the material aloud to yourself or discuss with others.

Computers: Read aloud any text that appears on the screen or discuss it with others.

Hands-On Activities: Talk about the activities while doing them or create your own auditory step-by-step directions.

Real-Life Experiences: Talk about the activities while doing them or create your own auditory step-by-step directions.

Learning from an Instructor: For a visual, tactile, or kinesthetic presentation, ask questions, discuss, orally describe the process, read aloud what you wrote, or verbally describe the moves step-by-step.

Superlink: Auditory Right-Brain Learners:
Media Type:
Written Material: Make a imaginary movie and hear the narration or dialogue spoken with expression, sound effects, or music to accompany the text, or invent rhymes, raps, songs, or rhythmic poetry about the material.

Graphic Material: Create rhymes, raps, songs, mnemonics, or poetry to help you comprehend the material; discuss the material with others, giving the global overview first.

Audio-Visual Material: If visual or auditory material is only the written or spoken word, add sound effects or read it with expression, while creating songs, rhymes, raps, or mnemonics to go with the material.

Computers: For materials with only written text or the spoken word, add sound effects or music, or read aloud with expression, using entertaining tones of voice

Hands-On Activities: For visual, tactile, or kinesthetic activities, make a colorful mind map and add sound effects or music or talk about it with others, using entertaining tones of voice.

Real-Life Experiences: For visual, tactile, or kinesthetic real-life experiences, make a colorful mind map and add sound effects or music, or talk about it with others, using entertaining tones of voice.

Learning from an Instructor: For a visual, tactile, or kinesthetic presentation, convert it into a movie in your mind, imagining the narration or dialogue with expressive tones of voice, sound effects, and/or music, and/or talk about it with others, using associations, mnemonics, poetry,raps, rhymes, or songs.

Superlink: Tactile Left-Brain Learners:
Media Type:
Written Material: Copy material or do note taking in your own hand or type it.

Graphic Material: Write a description of the graphics in your own hand, type it, do note taking, or make a model and label the components.

Audio-Visual Material: Do note taking and/or do the hands-on step-by-step process.

Computers: For graphics, write descriptions in your own hand, do note taking or type them out, or do the hands-on step-by-step process.

Hands-On Activities: This is ideal for tactile left-brain learners. Use a step-by-step approach and put it into words.

Real-Life Experiences: For visual, auditory, or kinesthetic activities, do note taking, and involve feelings.

Learning from an Instructor: For visual, auditory, or kinesthetic instruction, do note taking, perform hands-on activities, and involve your feelings.

Superlink: Tactile Right-Brain Learners:
Media Type:
Written Material: Draw, sketch, or make graphics, in color, to illustrate the words.

Graphic Material: Copy or draw the visuals or do a hands-on activity related to it; involve your feelings.

Audio-Visual Material: Draw, sketch, diagram, or make graphics, in color, or do a hands-on activity related to the audio-visual material.

Computers: Convert any written text from computers into graphics. If already in graphic form, copy it by drawing in color.

Hands-On Activities: This is ideal for tactile right-brain learners. Use a global approach beginning with the big picture or overview first.

Real-Life Experiences: Make color sketches or mind maps with illustrations to remind you of the experience.

Learning from an Instructor: Make sketches or colorful pictorial diagrams or mind maps of the presentation.

Superlink: Kinesthetic Left-Brain Learners:
Media Type:

Written Material: Act out the words in a step by-step way or imagine the action in your mind, feeling it in your muscles.

Graphic Material: Physically act out the graphic representation or imagine the action in your mind in a step-by-step way, while feeling it in your muscles.

Audio-Visual Material: Dramatize or imagine acting out the action in your mind, feeling it in your muscles, in a step-by-step way.

Computers: Physically act out the written text or graphics shown on the computer, or imagine doing the action, while feeling it in your muscles, in a step-by-step way.

Hands-On Activities: Visual, auditory, or tactile activities need to be carried out physically, or imagine doing the action in your mind, feeling it in your muscles, in a step-by-step way.

Real-Life Experiences: Ideal for kinesthetic left- brain learners. Use as a step-by-step approach and put it into words.

Learning from an Instructor: For visual, auditory, or tactile presentations, carry them out physically or imagine the action in your mind, feeling it in your muscles, in a step-by-step way, putting in into words.

Superlink: Kinesthetic Right-Brain Learners:
Media Type:
Written Material: Physically act out the words or imagine doing the action in your mind, feeling it in your muscles.

Graphic Material: Physically act out the graphic representation or imagine doing the action in your mind, feeling it in your muscles.

Audio-Visual Material: Carry out the actions physically or imagine the action in your mind, while feeling it in your muscles.

Computers: Written text or graphics need to be physically carried out, or imagine the action in your mind, feeling it in your muscles, with freedom of movement and imagination.

Hands-On Activities: For visual, auditory, and tactile activities, participate in the experience physically or imagine doing the action, feeling it in your muscles, with freedom of movement and imagination.

Real-Life Experiences: This is ideal for kinesthetic -brain learners. Use a global approach, beginning with the big picture, main idea, or overview.

Learning from an Instructor: For visual, auditory, or tactile instruction, physically act it out or imagine doing the action in your mind, while feeling it in your muscles, with freedom of movement and imagination.

In summary, each type of instruction and learning material can be made suitable for any type of learner.

There is no reason for books and graphic materials to be made only for visual people; books can be produced to appeal to auditory, tactile, and kinesthetic people who are either left brain or right brain or both. As a consultant and a writer of learning materials for many years, I have developed programs that deliver instruction through the medium that matches the learners' best superlink reading comprehension and learning style and brain style. For example, I created an entire pre-K, K-12, college and adult reading program, called Keys to Reading Success and Superlinks to Accelerated Learning with lessons in all eight superlink styles so everyone can improve reading comprehension to excel in reading, reading and listening comprehension, vocabulary, phonics, fluency, memory, note taking, study skills, and test-taking skills. Any medium can be converted to match the learner's reading comprehension style.

Exercise: Review the chapter on your superlink and then use the above information to find your best media of instruction and materials that matches your superlink reading comprehension style. Take notes of all the instructional methods and media materials that match your best reading comprehension and learning style and brain style to improve comprehension. Remember, if you are a combination of superlinks, select media materials from different parts of the above information, since you have two or more best superlink reading comprehension and learning styles and brain styles combinations.

The Learning Environment You Need

Your learning environment refers to where you will work, read, or study: the conditions in the room and other stimuli that can enhance or inhibit your ability to comprehend what you want to learn. You may have set yourself up with the right delivery of instruction and the right materials, but if your environment causes you discomfort or distractions it will be harder to concentrate. To improve reading comprehension to accelerate learning you want to eliminate as many steps that block your progress as possible.

When you set up your own environment, you can control your circumstances. But when you are in a training or class situation, you may not have control over your environment. Thus, you may have to ask the instructor for some assistance in making some adjustments in the environment, or use coping techniques to help you adapt to the situation.

Below is a list summarizing the best learning environment to improve reading comprehension for each superlink, followed by coping skills for adapting a noncompatible environment into one that is compatible for you.

Superlink: Visual Left-Brain Learners:
Best Learning Environment:

- Written material and the speaker are clearly visible.
- No visual clutter or disorganization.Printed material is neat and free of errors.Can work with or without music or auditory distractions because they can tune it out.
- Room is complete with filing systems, visual organizers, time schedules, calendars, and clocks. The instructor arrives on times and finishes on time.

Coping Strategies to Adapt a Noncompatible Environment:

- Try to sit close to the front to see posted visual materials.Keep your own area neat and organized. Offer to clean up, organize, and decorate the rest of the room. Correct errors in printed material.
- Request a time schedule. Wear a watch. Offer to be a timekeeper.

Superlink: Visual Right-Brain Learners
Best Learning Environment:

- Graphic or written material and the speaker are clearly visible.
- Visually attractive, colorful, and creative environments.
- Can work with or without music or auditory distractions because they can tune it out.
- Flexible schedule allows you to come and go at varying times.

Coping Strategies to Adapt a Noncompatible Environment:

- Sit near the front to see posted visual graphic materials.
- Keep your own area colorful, well designed, and attractive.
- Offer to decorate the area of the room at which you have to look.
- Use a color-coded, decorative calendar to artistically track your deadlines. Put up sticky-note messages to attract your attention and remind you of deadlines and due dates.

Superlink: Auditory Left-Brain Learners:
Best Learning Environment:

- You can listen to others and discuss your own ideas.
- Only one auditory stimulus at a time. No music in the background while studying or reading.
- Silence for reading or studying.
- Orderly environment has filing systems, organizers, and time schedules.
- Instructor gives out schedules. Comes on time and finishes on time.

Coping Strategies to Adapt a Noncompatible Environment:

- Sit with someone who will discuss the topic with you.
- Sit where you can hear the speaker well.
- Stay away from areas with noise distraction
- Bring headphones or earplugs to tune out music or distracting sounds when reading or studying.
- If you need to talk to yourself or read aloud, sit in an area where you will not disturb others. (Most likely

the only ones who will be disturbed are other auditory people.)

- Ask for a time schedule. Wear a watch.
- Offer to be a timekeeper.

Superlink: Auditory Right-Brain Learners:
Best Learning Environment:

- The sounds in the environment are pleasant.
- Sounds are harmonious with one another, for example, music combined with natural sounds.
- Talk is kept to a minimum, with key points emphasized.
- Flexible time schedule.
- Speaker is clearly audible and speaks with good expression.
- Absolute quiet for studying.
- No music in the background while studying or reading.

Coping Strategies to Adapt a Noncompatible Environment:

- Listen to music while doing work that does not require abstract thinking in the form of words.
- Sit where you can hear the speaker clearly.
- Avoid areas with noise distraction.
- Sit with someone who can repeat key points and verbal directions slowly and repeatedly, if needed, until you understand them.
- Bring headphones or earplugs to tune out distractions.
- If you need to talk to yourself, read aloud, or make your own sound effects, sit in an area where you will

not disturb others. (Most likely the only ones who will be disturbed are other auditory people.)

Superlink: Tactile Left-Brain Learners:
Best Learning Environment:

- Environment is physically and emotionally comfortable.
- You can sit next to people you like. You know the schedule and a clock is available.
- Room is organized and neat, where you can easily grab what you need.
- You are permitted to write, draw, and doodle as you listen or read.
- Can work or without music you like.
- Instructor has a positive communication style, using praise and positive words and positive nonverbal communication.

Coping Strategies to Adapt a Noncompatible Environment:

- Sit in a comfortable seat or bring a cushion or pillow to make uncomfortable seats feel better.
- If you do not like air-conditioning or heat, sit far from the ventilators or blowers. If you do not like sun glare, avoid sitting in the line of sunlight.
- If you like sun, or need a view of greenery or a peaceful setting, sit near the window.
- Select a location where you feel emotionally comfortable. Sit near people you like.
- Ask for a time schedule. Wear a watch. Keep an organizer for your papers.
- Keep notepaper and pens available. Sit where

doodling, writing, or touching objects does not bother the instructor or others.

- If you need music you like to work, bring headphones so as not to disturb others.

Superlink: Tactile Right-Brain Learners:
Best Learning Environment:

- Use comfortable seats. (Some may like to stretch out on the floor or couch, sit on a desktop, or recline or stretch out in their seats.)
- Physically and emotionally comfortable environment.
- You can sit near people you like and stay far away from people who you think do not like you. You are allowed to doodle, draw, or sketch.
- You can work with or without music, but it needs to be music you like.
- Flexible schedule.
- Instructor is someone you like and admire.

Coping Strategies to Adapt a Noncompatible Environment:

- Select your own seating to be physically or emotionally comfortable. Bring a pillow or cushion if the seat is uncomfortable.
- If you like scenery, sit near a window. Sit near or away from heaters, air-conditioners or sun-glare, if they make you uncomfortable, depending on your comfort level.
- Sit near someone you like. Avoid sitting near people who make you feel uncomfortable or upset.
- Keep drawing paper, colored pens, or markers for doodling and sketching, and sit where this does not distract others.

- If you like music to keep you feeling relaxed and positive, bring headphones so as to listen and not disturb others.
- Keep a color-coded calendar or use sticky-notes as reminder of time.
- Keep objects or belongings that make you feel good to touch on your desk or table. Give your desk or area a personal touch.

Superlink: Kinesthetic Left-Brain Learners:
Best Learning Environment:
- Plenty of space to stretch out and move around standing up
- You can get out of your seat or work Comfortable seats.
- White boards or flip charts allow you to stand up and write.
- Neat, organized surroundings. Time schedules.

Coping Strategies to Adapt a Noncompatible Environment:
- Sit near the back of the room so you can move around without distracting anyone.
- If you have to sit to work, use a chair in which you can lean back, stretch out, wiggle, or move a lot.
- Ask for a time schedule. Wear a watch.
- Bring a challenging game or activity or something to do quietly at your seat if you get bored after finishing work earlier than others and have to wait for the next part of the lesson.
- If you like music, bring headphones so as not to disturb others.

- Do arm or leg exercises at your seat if you get bored or restless.
- When studying, stay in a study carrel or put up a book or divider to block out the distraction of others' movements, or face a wall.

Superlink: Kinesthetic Right-Brain Learners:
Best Learning Environment:

- Enough space to move around and stretch out.
- You can get out of your seat or work standing up.
- Room has comfortable places to stretch out on the floor or couch, and if sitting is required, use chairs on which you can lean back, stretch your legs, wiggle, or move.
- You can play learning or movement games.
- You are permitted to work with or without music.
- When studying, sit at a study carrel or have a divider to block out the view of others' movements and activities.
- White boards, flip charts, or smart boards allow you to stand up and write.
- Flexible time schedule, and if work is done, allowed to leave early or keep working, if you want, well past the finishing time.
- Competitions, rewards, and awards for achieving a goal.

Coping Strategies to Adapt a Noncompatible Environment:

- Select a place where you can move around without disturbing others, preferably at the back of the room.
- Make sure if you have to sit, the seat allows you to lean back, stretch your legs, wiggle and move around.

- Bring a challenging game or activity, or something to do quietly when bored while waiting for the next task if you finish before the others.
- If you like music while learning, listen using headphones so as not to disturb others.
- Work at a study carrel or use a book or divider to block out distractions from others' movements or actions.
- Keep a color-coded calendar or use sticky-notes as reminders of time schedules.

Exercise: Use some of the above suggestions for your superlink reading comprehension and learning style and brain style and apply them to comprehending any subject quickly.

CHAPTER 21:

HOW TO LEARN TO IMPROVE AND INCREASE READING COMPREHENSION AND LISTENING COMPREHENSION USING YOUR BEST SUPERLINKS READING COMPREHENSION LEARNING STYLE AND BRAIN STYLE

In Chapter 20, you learned how to receive information in the fastest, most natural manner through your superlink. The next step is to improve reading comprehension and listening comprehension to ensure that you understand or comprehend the material. Think of it as having a delivery person get past the checkpoints in a high-security building. Using the best and fastest route, the letter is delivered. The next question is, Do you understand what the message says? Understanding the message when you read is called reading comprehension.

Grasping the message when you listen is called listening comprehension.

We may have material conveyed to us through our best learning style, but without training, we still may not comprehend it, or we may comprehend only a portion of it. Comprehension, for either reading or listening, is a skill that can be learned. Think back to a test you may not have done well on, painful as the memory may be. Did you study hard only to score seventy-five percent, eighty-eight percent, or even way below sixty-five percent? What happened? You only comprehended a portion of the material you learned. You thought you studied hard. What was missing? You may not have learned the skill of reading or listening comprehension.

In many schools today, teachers continue to test students' reading comprehension and listening comprehension. The latest emphasis in schools is on close reading, where we read to gather and refer back to information in the text. How can a student do this without being taught how to comprehend? If they fail, teachers have them study again, retest them, and see what they score the second or third time around. Yet are they ever taught *how* to comprehend? We often think that reading comprehension or listening comprehension are genetically-transmitted traits with which we are born or which we pick up by osmosis. It is not: Reading comprehension and listening comprehension are learned, acquired skills. In this chapter, you will learn the secrets to increasing your reading comprehension and listening comprehension, and hopefully it will not remain secret anymore to you. From kindergarten and first grade up to college and at the adult level, everyone needs to learn how to comprehend, but many adults never learned reading or listening comprehension at all. So get ready for Reading and Listening Comprehension Made Easy 101!

Reading and Listening Comprehension Techniques for the Eight Superlinks

By now you have an idea that people with different learning styles and brain hemispheric preferences think differently, comprehend differently, and respond to the world in a different way. They also comprehend in a different manner. The following are reading comprehension techniques I have developed and used successfully with people of all learning styles and brain hemispheric preferences. If you use these techniques, your comprehension can improve drastically. Many people who were previously struggling with comprehension have become so successful through the use of these techniques that they can actually comprehend and remember one hundred percent of what they read. If this were taught in schools, even from kindergarten and first grade on, we would see higher comprehension achievement scores for all students and adults. For those who are good readers, you may already intuitively know how to comprehend everything you read. But there are millions of students and adults who struggle with reading. They may pick up the gist of what they read, but miss most of it. The exercise in this section is designed to sharpen your reading comprehension whether you are a good reader or you are one of the millions of adults who managed to make it through school—or even through graduate school—but who wished they had known a way to read better and comprehend more fully. Many adults who have successful careers are still not satisfied with their ability to fully comprehend and remember what they read. They feel they have to take a long time to make it through readings and have no memory of what they read.

Overwhelmed by the many professional journals or training materials they are required to read at the workplace, they are too embarrassed to tell anyone about their struggle or to seek help. With changes in the workplace where innovations require people to learn new skills for their current jobs, or with frequent job loss due to companies going out of business or downsizing, people must look for new jobs, which may require learning and comprehending an entirely new career. In addition, with an ever-increasing average life span, people are living well into their senior years and want to keep learning. With the current emphasis on keeping your brain and comprehension skills sharp, seniors in great numbers are engaged in ongoing learning, so these tools can help them continue to keep their brain active.

This chapter provides some tools to make reading easier for those who want to learn more quickly and easily but who have been previously slowed down by poor comprehension techniques.

The basic techniques for reading comprehension, which I have named experiential or virtual reality comprehension, are described below, followed by adaptations for the different superlinks learning styles.

Instructions for Reading a Passage to Improve Reading Comprehension: To begin this exercise, you will read a sample passage, phrase by phrase. You are going to imagine that you are a movie director and are going to convert the words into a movie or video. Your job is to set up the scene, guide the actors and actresses as to what they should be doing and what their facial expressions should be, control the sound, and direct the action. Pretend that the printed text is a screenplay you have to convert back into action. Did you ever realize that printed text is merely a transcription of imaginary or real-life events that have been converted into words so that those who were not on the spot could read it to find out what happened? Reading is converting words back into the actual experiences or ideas that the author is trying to convey. That is your job as an imaginary movie director—convert the words back into a movie. The following adaptations will be made by people with each superlink learning style. I have given each type of reading a name so we can refer back to them.

Visual Experiential Reading Comprehension—Left and Right-Brain: As you read, you will imagine yourself *seeing* the text convert into a movie on a screen. You will watch this movie in your mind, seeing the people, places, and things. The question to ask yourself after reading each phrase or sentence is: What am I *seeing* in my movie?

Visual left-brain people will attend more to the visual language described, the sequence of events, and the linear structure of what they are reading.

Visual right-brain people will visualize the colors, shapes, sizes, designs, patterns, and the expressions on people's faces.

Auditory Experiential Reading Comprehension—Left and Right-Brain: As you read, you will imagine yourself *listening* to the movie and *hearing* the dialogue and voices, sounds, and sound effects. You can also be the one reading the lines or carrying on the discussions. After reading each phrase or sentence the question to ask yourself is: What am I *hearing*, what *sounds* am I making, or what am I *saying* in my movie?

Auditory left-brain people will hear the words of the movie in their heads and get meaning from them with or without the images.

Auditory right-brain people will listen to the music and sound effects they create to go with the movie. They will hear the sounds of the words, tones of voice, environmental sounds, and musical accompaniment and background.

Tactile Experiential Reading Comprehension—Left- and Right-Brain: As you read, you will imagine yourself *feeling* the events of the movie as if they were happening to you. You will immerse yourself in the characters and feel their emotions. You will feel the sensation of touch on your skin, hands, or fingers, or how things feel to touch as if you were there. The question to ask yourself after reading each phrase or sentence is: What am I *feeling* or *touching* in my movie?

Tactile left-brain people will pay more attention to the feelings and emotions as expressed in words or to describing in words what things feel like to touch.

Tactile right-brain people will be more attuned to descriptions of nonverbal communication (such as facial expressions, tones of voice, and body language) and emotions experienced inferentially—implied by the words. They also will note how things feel like to touch and will describe what it was like using only brief feeling words rather than a lengthy verbal description.

Kinesthetic Experiential Reading Comprehension— Left- and Right-Brain: As you read, you will imagine yourself experiencing the action or doing the movement described in the movie. Become the actors or actresses and carry out the movements yourself. Make the movie come alive—at a physical level. The question to ask yourself after reading each phrase or sentence is: What am I *doing* or *experiencing* in my movie? Turn everything into an action that can be experienced in your muscles.

Kinesthetic left-brain people will be more attuned to the actions along with a verbal description of the action.

Kinesthetic right-brain people will act out the movie in their mind. They will convert everything into some movement that they can feel their muscles make, without needing a long verbal description. Only a few action words are needed.

Now let's learn how to use the experiential or virtual reality reading comprehension technique. Below is a sample reading passage, but *do not* read it until the instructions tell you to do so. For the moment skip down to below the passage and read it according to the How to Read the Sample Passage: Rapid Learning. This exercise will teach you how to read using full experiential comprehension or virtual reality reading comprehension.

Sample Passage: "Rapid Learning"

An eager young man desired a part-time job to help make his way through Stanford University. As he stood before Louis Janin one Friday morning, he was told there was only a stenographer position available.

- I'd love it! exclaimed the excited young man.
- However, I can't start until next Wednesday. Bright and early on Wednesday morning, the young man reported for duty.
- I like the promptness and enthusiasm, Janin assured the lad.
- I do have one question. Why couldn't you start on Monday?

- Well, you see, sir, I had to find a typewriter and learn how to use it, replied the young man—Herbert Hoover—who would later become president of the United States.

How to Read the Sample Passage Called "Rapid Learning"

Read the first few words of the above passage, An eager young man. Either with eyes opened or closed, ask yourself, one of the following questions according to your superlink learning style:

Visual Learner: What am I seeing on my movie screen now?

Auditory Learner: What am I hearing or saying in my movie now?

Tactile Learner: What am I (or the characters) feeling or touching in my movie now?

Kinesthetic Learner: What action or movement am I (or the characters) experiencing my muscles doing in my movie now?

Think of this as the opening scene of the movie. The first thing that will appear on the screen is an eager young man. Since you are the director, imagine a young man in your mind, any way you want, to begin with. Do not read ahead yet, but work with that one phrase. (Note: As you continue reading, the passage may describe him more specifically, which at that time you will then move to the next scene and alter that man to fit the new information provided in the text.) Some of you may imagine a tall man, a thin man, and so forth. Unless, and until, the passage describes the man further, imagine him any way you wish. It is helpful to populate the movie with people you already know, such as family, friends, co-workers, or famous personalities, such as athletes, movie stars, or performers, etc. How you imagine that man is based on your superlink learning style. If you are visual, see the man. If you use someone you know to play the part of the man, visualize the features, such as hair and eye color, size, or clothing worn. If you are auditory, you will hear the man talking or his voice quality, or have him produce sounds, such as humming, singing, or whistling, or whatever way you wish to hear him. You may also hear a narrator reading aloud the text in your movie. If you are tactile, you will imagine what the man is touching or doing with his hands, or how he is feeling. If you are kinesthetic, you will imagine him in motion, and feel that movement in your own muscles as if you were moving. Instead of a stationary man just standing there, a kinesthetic learner should imagine him bursting on the screen in motion, such as running, swimming, playing sports, driving a car, or anything involving large muscle movement.

Next, let's work on the word eager. As director, have the actor in the movie express eagerness according to your superlink learning style. For example, a visual learner should see the man showing an expression of eagerness of his face. An auditory learner should hear eagerness in his voice, or have him say something to express eagerness. A tactile learner should feel eagerness within himself or herself to identify with the character's emotion. A kinesthetic learner should act out something that relates to being eager, such as excitedly opening a wrapped birthday gift, eager to find out what it contains, or being pumped up about winning a football game.

Now, read the next group of words: desired a part-time job to make his way through Stanford University. Based on your superlink learning style ask yourself one of the following questions, What am I seeing (hearing or saying, feeling or touching, or what action am I doing or experiencing) on my movie screen now? Then describe to yourself as director what you want to appear on the screen to make that phrase come alive in your superlink style. If you are visual you may see, for example, a college student carrying books and rushing off after school to a small office. Auditory learners may hear him say to his friends, I have to get a job to pay for school, and then hear the sound of the car radio blasting as he drives to work. Tactile learners may feel the anxiety of needing a part-time job to make money to pay the bills. Kinesthetic learners may experience hopping in their car to drive to a part-time job, racing through the streets, feeling the sensation of steering the car and the twists and turns of the road as they sway from side to side. It's your movie. You have the basic words to work with, but since they mean different things to different people, your movie is totally yours. The author may have had one thing in mind, but when it is not fully described, then some portion is left to your imagination.

Suppose it is important for you to learn the words Stanford University, because that information is needed for a test you must take or information you must talk about at your job. If you are familiar with the college, then based on your superlink learning and brain style, see it, hear the sounds on campus, feel yourself as part of the student body, or perform an action such as playing on its sports team or doing a science experiment in one of its labs. If you are not familiar with this particular school, find an association that you already have in your mind that sounds like or is spelled like Stanford. Do you know a person by the name of Stan whom you can visualize? Or think of smaller words that are a part of a whole word, such as *stand* and *Ford*. If you are visual, see yourself standing next to a Ford automobile. If auditory, hear the engine of the Ford as you stand by it. If you are tactile, feel yourself standing as your hands open the driver's side door of the Ford. If you are kinesthetic, feel yourself standing next to the Ford, and then jumping in and driving it away. There are times when these small details may not be important, such as when you are reading for pleasure, but when you are going to be held accountable for what you read, these associations will help you retain the information long after you close the book. Doing this exercise with detailed information will sharpen your brain to comprehend better what you are reading at the moment, as well as develop neural pathways and more automaticity for improving reading comprehension for anything you read in the future.

Go on to the read the next group of words: As he stood before Louis Janin… Again, ask yourself, based on your superlink learning and brain style, What am I seeing (hearing or saying, feeling or touching, or what action am I doing or experiencing) on my movie screen now? As director, continue rolling your movie cameras along. Without any description of the man, Louis Janin, it is up to each reader to imagine what he is like in his or her own superlink learning style. Visual learners should picture him, auditory learners may hear his name being said or hear him talk or make sound effects, and tactile learners may feel what kind of personality he has or what mood he is in, or have him doing something with his hands, like shaking hands. Kinesthetic learners should have him do something in which his large motor muscles are in motion, and then feel themselves doing that same action within their own muscles, for example, running into the office. Again, to remember his name, think of a Louis you know personally, a famous personality, or someone from history by that name and imagine him in your movie. Janin may not ring a bell with you, so associate it with some similar-looking or – sounding word: Jan, Jani, Jan in a place. Insert the association, imagined in your own superlink learning style, into your movie as a flashback, thought bubble as in a cartoon, or cutaway to help you remember the person's name.

Take the next group of words, one Friday morning… Note that if there are a variety of images, you can sometimes break a sentence into phrases, but sometimes you can work with a whole sentence. The benefit of breaking a sentence up in the beginning stages of mastering this technique is that sometimes, when the sentence has too much going on in it, you tend to visualize only a part of it, skipping over some images.

Until you get used to this technique, imagine every word of the text. You will discover for yourself how much you can read at a time so you do not miss anything. Back to the words in the sample text, one Friday morning. What comes on your movie screen when you think of Friday morning? The visuals may see a group of people at the office reading the weekend entertainment section of the newspaper to plan their days off. The auditories may hear themselves discussing where they want to go Friday afternoon after work or the sound effects of a concert they plan to attend Friday night. The tactile may feel excitement over the upcoming weekend. The kinesthetics may be passing out tickets that they picked up for the friends at the office for a basketball game for the next day.

Next, the passage reads: …he was told there was only a stenographer position available. Go ahead and experience that in your own sensory modality on your movie screen. Based on your superlink learning style, you can see a stenographer at work, hear the sound of someone hitting the keys, feel the sensation of your fingers on the keys, or feel your arm movements as you strike the keys. Suppose you do not know what a stenographer is. What happens to your movie? As director, the actors and actresses are waiting around for you to direct' them to act out the scene. Without you knowing what a stenographer is, what happens to your movie? It stops. This means that to keep the movie rolling, so there is no gap in your comprehension, you need to find the definition of the word, act it out according to your superlink learning style (either seeing it, hearing it, feeling or touching something related to it, or doing an action) and inserting that back into the movie. Many gaps in our comprehension are caused by not knowing a word, skipping it, and wondering why we cannot comprehend totally what we read. To be prepared for such circumstances, you can use any of the following tools: use a dictionary (either a physical book or a dictionary on the Internet), ask someone, or use the feature in some of the eBook readers that allow you to highlight a word so the definition pops up. Finding the meaning of unknown words will help your comprehension of what you are currently reading and build your vocabulary so that the next time the word appears in text or conversation, you already have a movie image for it.

The story continues: 'I'd love it!' exclaimed the excited young man. Although this is an auditory scene and the auditory learners may hear the words in their movie, the visual learners may see the expression on the man's face, the tactile learners may feel the excitement of having a chance at the job, and the kinesthetic learners may experience themselves jumping up or hitting their fist into the air with a loud Yes!

The passage next reads, However, I can't start until next Wednesday. Ask yourself what you see (or hear or say, feel or touch, or what actions your experience doing) on your movie screen next. Are you visual learners seeing the man pointing to Wednesday on a calendar? Are you auditories hearing yourself sayWednesday, or associating it with a favorite talk show you listen to on Wednesdays? Are you tactile learners feeling yourself write the word Wednesday in your Day-Timer? Are you kinesthetics remembering Wednesday because it is the day you go to fitness class?

Read the rest of the paragraph by yourself, breaking it up as follows between the slashes: Bright and early on Wednesday morning, / the young man reported for duty. / I like the promptness and enthusiasm, 'Janin assured the lad. / I do have one question. Why couldn't you start on Monday? '/ Well, you see, sir, I had to find a typewriter and learn how to use it, '/ replied the young man—Herbert Hoover/—who would later become president of the United States.

As you read each of the above phrases, remember the question to ask yourself that applies to your visual, auditory, tactile, or kinesthetic superlink learning style. Remember, you will have to be thinking the question to yourself as you read without anyone else reminding you. The question is: What am I seeing (hearing or saying, feeling or touching, or what action am I experiencing doing) on my movie screen now? With practice, you will no longer need to ask this question in your mind; you will just automatically convert the words into the movie. Do not skip anything, because you will find that what you did not imagine in your mind may be lost even minutes after you read it. What you do imagine in your superlink learning style will be there long after you read the passage.

Now, prove to yourself how much of the passage you comprehend. Answer the following questions aboutyour movie. While you reply, give only the basic answer that appeared in the *printed* story and leave out the additional information you created and added to help you comprehend. Answer purely from memory without looking at the passage again. No peeking back!

Questions:
1) Who is this story about?
2) What was he looking for?
3) To what school did he go?
4) What day did he have the interview?
5) What part of the day did he have the interview?
6) Who interviewed him?
7) What position was available?
8) How did he feel about taking the position that was available?
9) What day did he want to start?
10) Why did he choose that day to start work?

Answers: (Note, you may have added the description you made in your mind to the answers, but the basic answers are below:
1) Possible answers: a young man, an eager young man, or Herbert Hoover
2) A part-time job, or a part-time job to help him through school

215

3) Stanford University
4) Friday
5) Morning
6) Louis Janin, or a man
7) Stenographer
8) He was excited, or he said, I'd love it.
9) Wednesday
10) He needed time to learn how to type.

The key to experiential reading comprehension is to visualize the passage as vividly as you can, using your best learning style. When you visualize and make it real, your brain is taking it in as if it were actually happening to you. We tend to comprehend events that seem real to us better than we comprehend those we read about.

Think of how real a dream seems. It is not really happening, but while we are experiencing it, it feels real to us. Those who can recall their dreams find that they can remember them as clearly as events in their lives. We can use that same mental ability to help us comprehend what we read for the purpose of learning. If we experience the passage as if it were really happening to us, we will comprehend and remember it better. Thus, visual learners will feel as if they really saw it, auditory learners as if they really heard it, tactile learners as if they really felt it, and kinesthetic learners as if they really did it. It is startling to see how people who were previously scoring anywhere from a D or F on comprehension tests in a wide variety of subjects, began to score an A when they used this method. They learned how to achieve total comprehension of whatever they read. Others, marveling at their friend's new ability often wanted to learn it, too. The beauty of the method is that it can be learned by anyone of any age.

Did you ever wonder how a teenager who loves sports can study for hours for a test and come home with a low grade, yet can rattle off every sports statistic of his or her favorite team or all the players and give you a detailed description of each of their games? Does he or she have a comprehension problem? Certainly not, as evidenced by his or her seemingly fantastic comprehension when it comes to sports. It is just that this material—action sports—may be compatible with his or her superlink learning style and brain style, while the material he or she is studying is not action-oriented. But anything can be converted to a medium he or she will understand. If the material were converted into action, then your teen would remember it as vividly as the sports event.

This method can work with *any* reading material, both fiction and nonfiction, such as information reading. The key is to convert anything you read into a video, DVD, or movie. Think about how many scientific documentaries you see on television. They even make movies, DVDs, and videos about math, language, history, and computers! When you read in these various content areas all you are doing is becoming the producer or director and making a movie out of the material. You can even do this with abstract subjects that do not even seem to have any action. We will now see how to use experiential reading with a technical passage provided below. The same technique can be used for reading texts in science, math, social studies, technology, and content that is not about people or action. Do not read the passage until you follow the directions below the passage called: How to Read the Sample Technical Nonfiction Passage: 'Photosynthesis.'

Sample Technical Nonfiction Passage: *"Photosynthesis"*

Photosynthesis is a biochemical reaction that occurs when a green plant takes in sunlight, carbon dioxide from the air, and water, and converts them using its chlorophyll to carbohydrates and oxygen.

How to Read the Sample Nonfiction Technical Passage: *"Photosynthesis"*

Start with the first phrase: Photosynthesis is a biochemical reaction that occurs when a green plant... If you know what photosynthesis is, ask yourself, How can I represent this on my movie screen so viewers will know what it is? What am I seeing (hearing or saying, feeling, or doing?) If you do not know what photosynthesis is, the passage cues you by saying a biochemical reaction which lets you know that the rest of the sentence will tell you what it is. If you first need to read the whole sentence to picture photosynthesis, then do so, or look it up in a dictionary. On their movie screen, the visual learners may see a green plant with thick leaves growing in their flower garden. The auditory learners may hear the sounds in the garden, with the birds chirping in the trees or bees buzzing around the garden. The tactile learners may feel themselves sunning themselves next to the plant on a warm summer day, enjoying the gentle breeze blowing. The kinesthetic learners may experience themselves digging in the garden.

Let's read on: takes in sunlight. What is happening in your movie now? The visual learners may see the sun's rays entering the green plant. The auditories may hear the words or a vibratory sound representing light waves reaching the plant. The tactile learners may feel the warm rays penetrate their skin. The kinesthetic learners may fly from the sun down to the plant.

Next it says, carbon dioxide from the air. How will you portray carbon dioxide on your movie screen? The visual learners may see the symbol CO_2 or a drawing of a molecule of one carbon atom and two (di) oxygen molecules. They may see a person who is exhaling carbon dioxide gas. The auditory learners may hear CO_2 or the sound of these molecules bouncing around. They may hear someone exhaling carbon dioxide. The tactile learners may feel themselves writeCO_2 or feel themselves as a carbon dioxide molecule floating gently in the air and suddenly being squeezed through a plant's soft leaves. The kinesthetic learners may imagine themselves writing, while standing up, the symbol CO_2 with their arm tracing it in the air or writing on a flip chart, or experience themselves bouncing around in the air, knocking into many other molecules, and then being forcefully sucked into the plant.

The reading continues: and water. What is on your movie screen now? The visual learners may see water as a blue lake surrounded by a green forest. The auditory learners may hear the sound of the water in the ocean crashing on the shore. The tactile learners may feel themselves floating peacefully in the ocean, enjoying the waves lapping against their skin. The kinesthetic learners may experience themselves surfing the waves in the ocean. Whatever it takes to comprehend what you read is fair game.

Next, it says: and converts them using its chlorophyll. Again, you may or may not know what chlorophyll is. If you don't know, what happens to your movie? You cannot make an image for that scene and now have a gap in your movie.

The viewers are suddenly lost because the screen went blank. This shows what happens when we skip over vocabulary words we do not know. There is suddenly a gap in our understanding. At this point, what you need to do is to look up the word.

Get a dictionary, use a glossary in the text or look it up on an online dictionary on the Internet to find out, on the spot, what it is. If you wait, you may forget to look it up, and when you look it up later it is out of context and will not be as meaningful. If you stop and look up an unknown vocabulary word at the point that it enters the scene in the movie, you will comprehend it because you actively directed it in your movie, and then it makes sense in the context. Let us look up chlorophyll first, so we can proceed with the movie. We look in a glossary and find that chlorophyll is green material in the tissues of plants used for photosynthesis. Now back to our movie. Visual learners may see little green particles in the leaf of the plant taking in carbon dioxide and water, letting the sun cook them together. The auditory learners may hear the little green particles vibrating the carbon dioxide and water as it does its conversion process. The tactile learners may feel like they are the chlorophyll, opening their hands to hold the incoming carbon dioxide and water, and feel the warmth of the sun. The kinesthetic learners may experience themselves sucking in the carbon dioxide and water, and when the sun bombards them, shaking them at high speed to convert them.

Next, we read: into carbohydrates. How will you portray carbohydrates in your movie now? The visual learners may see a plate full of carbohydrates. The auditory learners may hear the sound of someone crunching carbohydrates. The tactile learners may feel themselves eating carbohydrates, enjoying their taste and the sensation of their texture in their mouths. The kinesthetics learners may feel themselves eating some carbohydrates as they rush out to the gym to exercise.

Finally, we conclude the passage by reading: and oxygen. How will you show that in your movie to viewers in the audience? Visual learners may show themselves outdoors, taking a deep breath, and breathing in little oxygen molecules that they see on their screen. The auditory learners may hear themselves take that deep breath. The tactile learners will feel the oxygen entering their mouths and traveling down their windpipe and into their lungs. The kinesthetic learners may be running on the track and taking in deep gulps of oxygen, feeling the muscles of their chest expand as they breathe in.

Now, let's do a reading comprehension practice test on this passage. Answer without looking back at the passage. As a question comes up, relax and recall the movie you created. Do not try to force yourself to comprehend the words—just let the images come up.

- Visual learners will relax and say, What did I see?
- Auditory learners, What did I hear?
- Tactile learners, What did I feel?
- Kinesthetic learners, What did I do?

Questions:
1) What is this passage about?
2) What do green plants do?
3) What does the green plant need for the process of photosynthesis to take place?
4) What does chlorophyll do?
5) What two things do green plants give off after chlorophyll converts the ingredients it took in?

Answers:
1) photosynthesis (or the description of photosynthesis);
2) take in sunlight, carbon dioxide from the air, and water and converts them using its chlorophyll to carbohydrates and oxygen;
3) chlorophyll (or sunlight, carbon dioxide and water);
4) convert sunlight, carbon dioxide, and water into oxygen and carbohydrates;
5) oxygen and carbohydrates.

You can see how this process works well with technical material. Anything can be converted into a movie, and you will comprehend it much better because the reading material becomes an activity you experienced through your best learning style.

You may also understand from the above example why we have to read a passage in small parts. Remember, whatever we do not portray in our movie may be forgotten. Technical reading requires more careful attention than pleasure reading. Since there are so many technical details, we need to take the time to image everything. If we do not, we may take double, triple, or quadruple the time to learn by reading this passage over and over in the hopes that we will comprehend each detail. But by experiencing it as a movie or as live action, we can comprehend it with even one careful or close reading.

You may say that this feels like it is taking you longer to read. First of all, this was a demonstration to teach you how to do it, so I was talking you through the process. Second, because I addressed four different learning styles, it felt longer—but you will only be asking yourself the question related to your superlink learning style. Third, you will be asking the question in your own mind, which is faster. Fourth, after practicing for a few days or weeks you will not need to verbalize the question anymore; you will automatically convert the words into images. Think of it as taking a bite of food, chewing, and swallowing—you take a bite of the word, digest it, and get the image. Fifth, the process of reading a word and getting an image will not be two separate occurrences; they will happen simultaneously. You will reach a point when you read the word and the images appear immediately, and you can clip along at a fast pace, getting a series of images without even being aware of reading the words. That is what good readers do.

Reading comprehension is something *everyone* can learn to do. Whether we call it improving our reading comprehension of what we read or close reading or reading for information, with practice you will not even be aware that you are reading, but will instantly be absorbed in the movie you made in your mind as you turn the pages of the book. You may never have learned to read this way and suddenly find how enjoyable it is to have an entire movie playing out in your head as you turn the pages. This is why there are millions of people who enjoy reading—they are getting the experiential movie in their heads. Did you ever hear some people say they prefer reading the book to seeing the movie of the same title? Why? First, because they experience the book as a movie, imagining the scenes based on their own experiences. After all, that is what the filmmaker or screenwriter is doing. They have taken the same script you are reading in book form and converting it to images on the screen. When you read the book yourself, you are the director and can determine the actors, actresses, and scenery, even putting yourself and people you know into the story and living it as if you are there. That is why it is so engrossing and engaging for some people to read and why they cannot put a book down until they are finished. Second, in a book you also experience the feelings and thoughts of the characters, while on a movie screen you can only infer them from the actors' facial expressions, tones of voice, or actions. We can relate to the characters, share their experience, and know that others go through many of the same emotions and thoughts that we have. We can also find solutions to our problems as they work through theirs.

Exercise: Practice Experiential Reading Comprehension with Your Own Reading Material:

For the purpose of the initial exercise, chose a fictional piece with descriptions of a person doing something.

Take a paragraph or two and read it in the way described in the two sample passages above. Ask yourself what is happening in your movie and either describe it in your head or aloud. If you want a partner to help you, have your partner ask you, What is happening in your movie? Describe the scenes phrase by phrase or sentence by sentence. Visual learners will see it, auditory learners will hear it, tactile learners will feel it, and kinesthetic learners will act out the action. If you are a combination of superlink learning styles, you will combine several senses. After reading the page, ask yourselves questions to recall what you read, or have someone ask questions about the passage for you. If you cannot think of the questions to ask, just relate back everything you remember that happened in your movie, and then check your response against the text to verify how much you comprehended.

Eliminating Blocks to Reading and Listening Comprehension

There are several blocks to reading and listening comprehension that hinder us as we read or listen. Many people struggle to read and go through life never learning how to eliminate these blocks. They are: being unable to associate new learning with the knowledge they already have; misunderstanding the terminology and vocabulary; and being unable to break words down into syllables to figure out the longer words. This next section will take each of these factors and show you how to eliminate these problems to help accelerate your learning.

Hooking Information into Our Prior Knowledge

When we are first faced with information, the brain perceives it either visually, auditorially, tactilely, or kinesthetically, and asks one question: Do I recognize this information? It searches its database of memories and comes up with three possible answers:

1) Yes, I already know this information.
2) No, I do not know this information at all.

It is similar to something I know, but different in some ways.

If the brain already knows the information, it just reconfirms it; it does not have to put in any further effort to alter its knowledge base. For example, while shopping in the grocery store we see the cauliflower stand and recognize cauliflower. We do not give it much thought because we already know it.

If the brain decides that it does not know the information at all, then it has more work to do, slowing down the process. It has to create a new memory connection for the information and learn more about what it is. In most cases, the brain will try to avoid this step and stay with the step above—linking it to something it already knows because it is easier. For example, you are in the grocery store and you see a vegetable whose shape, color, and name you never saw or heard of before. You have no idea of what it tastes like, how to prepare it, where it comes from, and what it is used for. You have a lot of work to do to find additional data about this vegetable. Chances are if you came across the word for that vegetable in a text, you may recall seeing it, but have no idea what it is, and could not easily comprehend that text. It would be a lot of easier if someone said to you, This vegetable is like squash, tastes like squash, but differs in shape and color. Then it would be easier for you to hook it into your memory bank with data on squash.

If the brain finds that the information is similar but not exactly like what is in its memory, it will evaluate the ways it is similar and how it differs. It will then link the new information to that specific memory that is similar, making an association with what it knows. The brain cuts down its work of assimilating the new information because it says, Oh, it is just like that other thing I already have in my memory. I only have to understand what makes it different. It is easier to learn information associated with what we already know because we only need to accommodate the differences.

For example, we see green cauliflower in the store. We stop and think, Oh, this is something new. It looks like cauliflower in shape but like broccoli in color. You read the sign and it says, Broccoflower. You now alter your mental database to accommodate a new form of cauliflower that is green like broccoli, or a new form of broccoli that looks like cauliflower, depending upon how you look at it.

Thus, the first step in comprehension is to make associations between the new material and the old. When we are learning something new, we want to find a way to connect it to our prior knowledge. Think of it as a computer database in which certain programs already exist in the hard drive. If we try to open a file in a program not installed on the hard drive, the computer would not be able to recognize and read it. We would have to convert the format of the program into what is on the hard drive to be able to comprehend it.

Understanding New Terminology and Vocabulary

We need to use terminology or vocabulary to understand new data. We may encounter a new object, concept, or idea, but unless we can use terminology or vocabulary that we already have in our brain, we will not understand the meaning or function of the new data. It is like learning a word from another language. The word is only a collection of sounds and letters until we know its definition. Only then can we interpret the information and comprehend it.

If we are learning the material on our own and we come across an unfamiliar word, we need to first define it and then try to connect it to something similar in our memory. To define the new information, we may need to look in a reference source such as dictionary, glossary, or encyclopedia, either in a physical book form or online. If it is a term found while reading a physical book or eBook, then the first time the information appears we need to look back to previous pages where it will usually be defined. There, we can find written examples or graphic illustrations. In an eBook, we can click on a link and an elaboration or definition of the word appears. We can also ask someone what it means.

We need to take responsibility for finding the definition. Often, when we do not know a new term, we just skip over it for one reason or another. This is how we develop faulty reading comprehension; by not bothering to find out what each new bit of information means, we create a gap in our understanding. Suppose that information turns up again over and over in the material. Our comprehension continues to drop because further knowledge is dependent upon the terms we skipped. This could happen when we are reading, listening to a lecture, or doing a procedure. If we do not take the time to understand the meaning of each term, we will fumble because we will not understand the material.

Hopefully, when we are learning from an instructor or from print material, audio-visual or digital material, or computers, the presentation will adequately ensure that new information is properly defined for you. However, there is no way to know what the learner already knows from his or her prior education. Thus, it is up to us as learners to ask for clarification when something is new or unfamiliar, and learn how to look up information in reference materials ourselves.

As you learn, you should keep track of any vocabulary or terminology you do not understand. If you are visual, tactile, or kinesthetic, write it down as a reminder to look up the definition at the first available opportunity. If you are auditory, stop and ask questions as soon as it is feasible. You can then use your superlink learning style to define the word in the following ways:

Visual Left-Brain: Read the word and its definition. Find or make a list of these words so they can be seen or reread.

Visual Right-Brain: Find or make a diagram or mind map of the word, the definition, and a pictorial clue.

Auditory Left-Brain: Talk about the word and its definition and use it in a sentence.

Auditory Right-Brain: Talk about an association between the sound of the new word with a word you already know. Then, make up an imaginative story that connects the old word you know, the new word, and its definition. For example: *cacophony* meanshorrible sound or noise. Think caco sounds like *cackle*, a word I already know, which is a sharp, broken noise or cry that hens make, or a laugh imitating a hen. If you did not know that phon is derived from the Greek word for *sound*, you could also think of *telephone*. In your imaginary story you may pick up a telephone and hear the horrible cackling of hens on the other end, and connect it to the word's meaning of horrible sound. Thus, when you hear the word *cacophony* you will think about hens cackling on the phone, and remember it means horrible noise or sound.

Tactile Left-Brain: Write the word and its definition in a list and for each word write an association connecting it with your feelings or an emotional situation from your past. Write the new words on a card and the definition on other cards, and use your hands to arrange the cards to match. Play games with the new words involving your hands.

229

Tactile Right-Brain: Write the word and its definition in a colorful, creative way and draw a picture to go with it, or make a mind map. Connect the word to feelings you have about the word or some situation in the past involving emotions that you associate with the word. Visualize yourself recreating a movie of the circumstance in your mind, using the new word in its associated situation.

Kinesthetic Left-Brain: Take large paper and, while standing up, write the word and its definition in a list and relate it to an action to go with the meaning. Act out the word in a situation in which it would be used. If that is not possible, imagine yourself acting out an action situation that involves the word. Do a movement activity (walking, jogging in place, tossing a ball in the air) as you read through your list of words and their definitions.

Kinesthetic Right-Brain: Take large paper and, while standing up, write the word in large size and in color with the definition arranged as a mind map with an action drawing in color accompanying the meaning. Act out the word in a situation that relates to the word.

Imagine yourself acting out a situation that would involve the word, or make up an imaginative action story using the new word, other words you already know that sound similar, and the definition of the word. Do a physical activity, such as bouncing a ball, jogging in place, or pedaling on an exercise bike, etc., while reading back your word and the meanings.

You will find that it will be easier to learn the meanings of unfamiliar words and terms when you do so in your best superlink learning style.

The techniques in this chapter can be used for several purposes. They can eliminate blocks to reading comprehension due to not knowing how to read all the sounds in English. They can also be applied to learning a different language. Finally, they can be used to learn symbols in various technical languages, such as computer languages, science, math, or any other fields that have specialized symbols.

One difficulty that prevents us from understanding the meanings of the words we read, either in English or in another language, is that we may not be able to say a word because we do not know what sounds the letters make. English is a complicated language because one letter may have many phonetic sounds.

There are a surprising number of adults whom I have met, many with high school and even college degrees, who cannot properly read passages aloud that contain multisyllabic words or a higher-level vocabulary because they do not know phonics or how to read the more complicated phonetic letter patterns in those words. The same holds true for many high school and college students who struggle with reading text at those levels.

Many of them find their comprehension suffers because they end up skipping over the hard words. In some languages, you only have to learn one sound for each letter, but, in English phonics, did you know that there are more than twenty-five ways to read and spell the letter *o*, depending upon which letters it is next to? For example, *o* can be pronounced and combined with different letters to give us: *hot, rope, go, toe, boat, book, boot, out, through, bought, dough, rough, could, cow, row, other, or, tore, door, soar, doll, troll, hole, goal, oil, and boy*, etc. If someone does not learn all the possible combinations for each vowel sound, it is easy to misread words. Thus, many people have reading problems both in English and in other languages because they have not learned all the letter-sound, phonics, or phonetic combinations. How did this happen? A startling number of students in upper grades and college, as well as adults, cannot convert the letters they see on the page into the correct sounds because they never learned or mastered the phonics or letter-sound relationships or phonetic patterns. Often adults notice this problem for the first time only when they are given technical reading material, professional journals, or training materials to read at the workplace, or they take a test for their job, and they suddenly realize they do not have all the tools to tackle the task. They considered themselves readers, and often did not notice the problem because many popular books, magazines, and newspapers are written at a lower reading level. These adults may have previously figured out words only from their contexts. Sometimes they may have been accurate and at other times they may have been far from the right word due to guessing the actual word. As a result, they either read the wrong word and did not comprehend the reading material, or they skipped the word and were left with a gap in their reading comprehension.

Some may use the letters they see, but when they do not know the correct sounds, their brain may do a word search and pop out with a word made of a mix of those letters, but which is not the actual word. If they do this, they generally are guess-reading the word and it is often not the accurate word. The results of these various strategies is that they either have read the wrong word and do not comprehend what they read accurately, or they have a gap in their knowledge because they skipped the word.

Some people can comprehend what they read when they know all the words, but when they cannot read the words correctly, it seems that they have a comprehension problem. In fact, they may not have a reading comprehension problem; they have a letter- sound relationship or phonics problem. Someone may try to help them by giving endless comprehension exercises to boost their abilities in that area, but their problem is a different one—they need to learn how to read the words before they can answer questions based on what they actually read—not what they guessed they read.

If you find that you struggle with hard words, it may be because you do not know the correct pronunciation of some phonics patterns. If you do not have this difficulty, you can still apply the following section to learning the letter-sound relationships or phonics of English or any other language based on phonics patterns. If you have to learn a second language, you will accelerate your learning by using your best superlink learning style. To accelerate reading instruction, all the letter-sound relationships or phonics patterns should be taught in the first year, along with comprehension, vocabulary, and independent reading strategies. If, instead of just learning a few of the sounds in the first year of reading, students of all ages learned *all* the sounds in that first year, they would accelerate their reading abilities and comprehension as well as their speed.

Another factor that may have caused a problem with word reading is that many people did not grasp the sounds various letters made because the first time they learned it they were not taught it in their best learning style. Letter-sound relationships or phonics can be learned through one's best superlink learning style.

Entire schools and school districts who initially had two-thirds of their students not meeting state standards in reading due to their lack of knowledge of all the phonics patterns discovered that when students were taught phonics in an accelerated way through each student's best superlink learning style, the district or school rose to two-thirds of the students meeting and exceeding state reading standards in eight months or less (less than one school year.) The result of those initial errors in accurately reading the words caused gaps in their reading comprehension; however, when their word-reading ability improved, their comprehension scores also rose. When there are word-reading gaps, it makes a big, gaping hole in the imaginary movie readers make in their minds. Although some may use strategies, such as using the first letter of a word combined with the context to figure out what word makes sense, this may result in not actually reading the correct word, causing comprehension errors. This shows up as a critical problem when: a) the number of words at which the reader is guessing using only the context becomes too large and they no longer are reading the same exact passage that is printed; b) when tested, they guess the wrong word and do not answer the question correctly. (This can happen not only on straight reading comprehension tests, but in any content area subjects such as science, social studies, or math); c) they become so used to guess reading that when they enter the job market, someone discovers they misread directions or instructions critical to getting their job done accurately. Has it ever occurred to anyone that the reason why two- thirds of the nation's students struggle with reading, according to the United States Department of Education statistics, is that many cannot even read the words? We may think it is due to reading comprehension problems alone, but it could be that their comprehension is fine; it is their knowledge of vocabulary or ability even to read the words using phonics patterns that are lacking.

Some people may graduate school and still not know all the letter-sound relationships or phonics patterns, either because it was not taught, or if it were taught, it was not taught in their best superlink learning style. Some people might have been taught these letter- sound relationships only partially or piecemeal but did not learn *all* the phonics patterns. What this means is that you may learn a few phonics patterns in a first grade reading class, a few more in a second grade reading class, and some more in third grade, and the rest in the upper grades of elementary school. Yet children are exposed or asked to read to all letter-sound relationships or phonics patterns in written material from the very beginning years of school, including first and second grade. They are given books to read in which all the letter-sound relationships or phonics patterns of English appear. At the earlier stages, they can only sound out a few patterns they learned. They may pick up several hundred easy words by sight. However, what happens when they get a new and unfamiliar word? As long as they have a picture clue in young reader books in first and second grade, they can guess the meaning from context, but when the pictures become less and the number of new words increases dramatically, such as from third and fourth grade and higher, they have to guess from too many words from the context to even make sense of what they are reading. Thus, the earlier they are taught all the letter-sound or phonics patterns of English (or any other language based on phonics), the less gaps they will have in their reading and the more they will read fluently, comprehending fully what they read. If instead of just teaching a few of the sounds in first grade or in the first year of reading, students of all ages, including adults, learned all the sounds in their first year of study, they would accelerate their reading abilities, fluency, and reading comprehension, as well as their speed, and would not be slowed down by rereading the sentence repeatedly to guess the context. They also would not be slowed down because they failed a test and had to retake the course since they did not know how to read all the words!

The key to learning the letter-sound or phonics relationships the first time around is to learn it in your best superlink learning style. The following are techniques to use to learn the letter-sound or phonics patterns through each superlink learning style and brain style:

Visual Left-Brain Learner: Look at the letter printed on a page, a white board, or in a book, accompanied by a picture clue and an example word that begins with that letter. Play games that involve matching the letters or phonics patterns with words with that pattern. Do word searches with the letters and patterns. Play step-by-step word games and arrange letter tiles to form words.

Visual Right-Brain Learner: Look at the letter printed in a book, on a chart or poster, or on a white board, in color with an attractive design, along with a picture clue and example word. Notice the shape and patterns of the letter. Play games that involve matching the shapes of the letters or the patterns with words with the same pattern. Do word searches with the letters and patterns. Play imaginative word games with the letter tiles. Create your own words with the letters.

Auditory Left-Brain Learner: Look at the letter and say it aloud, along with looking at and saying words that start with that letter. Verbalize any rules for remembering the letter. Talk about the pen strokes needed to make the letter, such as *b* is a stick followed by a ball. Talk about the words in sentences. Narrate stories using the words in the sentences. Play oral word games in which you use the words.

Auditory Right-Brain Learners: Look at the letter and say it aloud in a rhythmic way. Look at and say any words that go with the letter in a rhythmic or rhyming way. Put it to music. Recite or sing a short jingle or make a rap song to help you comprehend the sound. For example, to learn that c has two sounds:

k and s, recite to a rap beat:
C can be a k as in the word catty,
And c can be an s as in the word city. Don't be confused
By all of these rules:
Put c before a, u, or o
To form a *cat* who is *cute* and *cool.*
Put a c before an e, i, or y
To drive to the *center* of the *city* on a *cycle.*

Another technique is to tell imaginative stories using words with those phonics or letter-sound patterns. Play auditory word games with the patterns.

Tactile Left-Brain Learner: Write the letter on paper or a white board, or write it in some other way; for example, in sand with your finger or tracing the letter on a desktop. Write any sample words to go with it and draw a picture clue that starts with that letter. Make words with the letter using letter cards. Write rules for pronouncing the letter. Type the words on computer. Tie words to your feelings by finding words for things or people you like that start with the letter. Write sentences connecting the words to your feelings.

Tactile Right-Brain Learner: Write the letter on paper or on a chart in bright colors in a decorative way. Draw a picture clue to go with it and write the word for the picture. Make an arts and crafts picture of the letter. Outline the shape with different colored markers or crayons. Type the words on computer. Find and write words for things or people you like to start with the letter and illustrate them. Write imaginative sentences or stories connecting the word to your feelings or sense of touch.

Kinesthetic Left-Brain Learners: Write the letter in the air in large print with the arm muscles of your writing hand, or write the letter on the wall with a flashlight using all your arm muscles. Stand up and write the letter in large size on a flip chart, chalkboard, or dry- erase white board. Use large three-dimensional letter blocks and move them around to make words. Draw the letters in chalk on the sidewalk about six feet tall, and walk along the letters, saying them as you go. Learn any rules for pronouncing the letter. Play step-by-step games to learn the patterns.

Kinesthetic Right-Brain Learner: Write the letter in the air with the arm you use for writing, or write it on the ceiling with a flashlight. Write the letter large while standing up at a flip chart and draw an action picture that starts with the letter. Use large three- dimensional letter blocks and move them around to make words. Walk along the letter drawn on a sidewalk while saying it and seeing it. Make the letter with your body while saying it and seeing it. Do an action that starts with the letter and say and see the letter as you do the action. As you say the letter and words that start with it, throw a basketball into a net, bounce a ball, or do some activity with your body. Hang up your letters and words where you can see them, and read the letter and matching words while doing an activity or your favorite hobby, such as pedaling on an exercise bike, walking around the room, hitting a golf ball, jumping rope, or throwing a basketball, etc. Give yourself points each time you read the word and make a basket. Reward yourself for a certain number of points. Play games to learn the patterns.

(These are only some sample activities for each superlink learning style. For more activities for each superlink learning style you can refer to the following resources, such as my other books: *Solving Your Child's Reading Problems*; *Your Child Can Be a Great Reader*; *The Fine Line between ADHD and Kinesthetic Learning: 197 Kinesthetic Activities to Quickly Improve Reading, Memory, and Learning*; *Kinesthetic Vocabulary Activities*; *Tactile Vocabulary Activities*; plus two Internet Software programs to learn to read and improve in reading comprehension, memory, phonics, fluency, vocabulary, study skills, note taking, and test-taking skills, in one's superlinks learning style and brain style, *Keys to Reading Success*™ and *Superlinks to Accelerated Learning*™ (www.readinginstruction.com). Those interested in learning reading techniques using superlinks learning styles and brain hemispheric preference styles can get more information, practice materials, and take workshops and courses from National Reading Diagnostics Institute and Keys Learning in Naperville, Illinois.

When you learn the letter-sound relationships or phonics patterns in English or another language through your correct superlinks learning style and brain style, learning is accelerated, easier, and more fun because you are working in your element.

What about Listening Comprehension?

The examples in this chapter describe comprehension tasks as related to reading, but listening comprehension involves the same skills. The same strategies for using our best learning style and brain style described in the above sections on comprehending what we read can be used to comprehend what we hear when listening to a speaker, either in person, through streaming audio or video on the web, in the movies, or on any digital audio or video device.

Pulling It All Together to Accelerate Progress in Improving Reading Comprehension

By involving your superlink learning style and brain style in using the reading and teaching strategies in this chapter, you can gain a fuller understanding while improving your comprehension of everything you read and hear, empowering you to comprehend and master the subject you are studying at an accelerated rate.

CHAPTER 22:

ACCELERATED LEARNING: A LIFE-LONG PLAN: APPLYING WHAT YOU HAVE LEARNED ABOUT IMPROVING READING COMPREHENSION TO ACHIEVE YOUR GOALS

In this new millennium, our concept of education and learning is rapidly changing. With the information explosion, we have access to every bit of information that exists in the world today. As our education system catches up to current technology, we will find that learning will no longer consist of memorization of textbooks in order to pass tests. We will discover that learning is a process of personal transformation along our life's journey to fulfill our goals and dreams and to contribute to making the world a more humane, more peaceful, and more satisfying place to live. Learning will become a tool for the attainment of our individual and collective destinies.

As we realize that we have only a given number of years to live and enough information in the world to occupy us for many lifetimes we will need to make choices as to what we want to learn and for what purpose. No one has the time to know everything there is to know. We must accept that fact and decide what portion of that vast ocean of knowledge we want to own. It will not be the same for everyone. As we have seen, people have different interests and talents. In this book, we have seen the vast differences that exist between the eight types of learners and the combinations of superlinks learning styles and brain styles and how our own unique skills contribute to the diversity and talent pool required to make this world function. Each superlink learning style and brain style plays a part in human interdependence and each style is as valuable as the next. We need to honor and respect our differences and use our combined talents to solve mutual problems facing our planet.

In this millennium, we will need to take charge of our own learning and education. As the job market changes with each new technological discovery, we need to keep pace with it and decide what we need to know, when we need to know it, and for what purpose. We will rely more and more on self-study and self-learning as we strive to compete with this ever-changing panorama of the modern world. We not only need to learn this for ourselves, but we need to teach these tools to children so they can be ready for whatever world faces them when they grow up.

The knowledge you gained in this book can empower you with the skill of knowing how to learn any subject quickly and to master it. To date, this is the most current technology available to us. With each passing year, more research findings and newer technologies will provide us with still more ways to accelerate our learning. Who knows—one day, we may have microchips or a pill with a memory chip implanted in us from which we can access all the world's knowledge!

We need to always stay open to new discoveries and new findings and add it to our existing knowledge to move forward. Until those new technologies are accessed, you have the tools in this book – tools that can empower you to learn any subject in the shortest possible time. If you did the practice exercises, you would already have used these tools to work through one subject that you selected as a practice case.

In the beginning of this book, you selected a subject to learn as you worked through the activities. You also had a goal or purpose for learning that subject. Think back to what that goal was. If you worked through all these practice activities, you would be well on your way to mastering your subject by using the tools provided in the book. You can now apply this to learn other areas. Take a moment and list other areas that you would like to learn. Then, go through all the exercise pages in the book to complete your personal plan for learning each of these subjects.

Many people think of learning as a dead-end road. They learn something and that is the end of it. Few people actually *use* what they learn. Many people take courses and never apply the material or skills they have learned to their lives. Twelve years of schooling, possibly sixteen or more if we go to training schools, colleges, or higher education, have conditioned us into taking courses, passing tests, and forgetting the material the following day. As a society, we have come to equate learning with passing tests and getting grades, diplomas, or certificates. However, the true nature of learning is a transformation into a better self, a higher self, a fully-developed self. As a by-product, we can put what we learned into the service of humanity at large and make the world a better place. Learning is a tool to help us achieve our goals and dreams.

The final step in accelerated learning by improving reading comprehension is to apply what we learned to our everyday lives. That is the best and fastest way to crown our learning and to ensure our mastery of the subject. Having reached the point where we have mastered a subject, we want to gain experience by applying what we learned to real-life situations. By doing so, we move forward on our life's journey to meet the goals we have set for ourselves.

If we are learning a skill for a current job or hobby, we are most likely going to apply what we learned on a regular basis. If we have learned a new subject unrelated to our current activities, the following are some examples of how we can apply these to everyday life:

Literature: Continue to read on your own; start a discussion group; keep a journal; and do your own writing.

Sports or dance: Find some friends or join a group to practice a sport or dance.

Using the Internet: Spend time daily surfing to locate websites related to your interests.

Carpentry: Start a small project, building something for your home or family or friends

Cooking: Invite friends over for a gourmet meal.

Marketing: Take a product your business produces and improve on marketing it.

Health: Set some personal health goals in the areas of diet, nutrition, fitness, or exercise; start a personal program for yourself or join a fitness club.

Quantum Physics: Find a laboratory to visit or work in, either part-time or as a volunteer so you can apply what you learned to research; join a book study group on the subject.

Golf: One of my next books deals with how to improve golf through your superlnks learning style and brain style so you can work with an instructor to improve your golf game in the way you need to learn.

Learning is more than studying for a test. Having passed our examinations or performance assessments and proven our knowledge of a subject or skill, we do not want to have wasted all that time and let our knowledge fade away with disuse. True, there may be subjects we had to take for which we had no use. Focus instead on those subjects that you chose to study as part of your life's work, goals, interests, hobbies, or talents. The process of accelerated learning is complete when we use what we learned right away.

In the past, learners used to do tons of practice activities, yet did not recall the subject when they were assessed months later because they did not apply what they learned. When they used their knowledge and skills in everyday life the material stayed in their long-term memory. The final stage in accelerated learning is to use what you learned in your daily life.

Accelerated Learning Begins Early

Jerome Bruner, the great educationist, taught that anything can be taught to anyone at any age if taught at his or her level. This one statement that I read when I was in college has guided my entire teaching career, and I have found it to prove true time and time again. By using the technology in this book, you can begin accelerating the learning of children from birth.

We have a misconception in our society that the very

young and very old are living in a state, unaware of what is happening around them. We let children lie in cribs or carriages for hours, unstimulated with no one to talk to them, no one to provide them with challenges, no one to expose them to life. For each hour they lie awake doing nothing, they lose an hour of learning time. It is the same with the elderly who are left to sit with nothing to do.

Learning begins at birth. When we expose children to mental stimuli in infancy and their toddler years, we help them develop talents and abilities early. From infancy, we can develop their whole brain, both left and right sides, and all four learning styles, visual, auditory, tactile, and kinesthetic, by exposing them to a rich environment filled with stimuli in each modality.

We need not wait until age five, when they enter kindergarten. As a society we need to extend education to infancy, training parents and communities to provide opportunities for early stimulation. Having work with gifted students, I found that a common thread in each of their upbringings was that their parents provided them with early language experiences, early reading experiences, and a wide range of experiences in math, science, music, art, sports, and hobbies as babies and toddlers.

Those children who are identified as gifted and talented or who have high IQs (intelligence quotients) are not necessarily genetically endowed; part of it is due to their upbringing—to what stimulus they were exposed. When I worked with gifted students I used to question their parents as to what they did with their children during their infancy to find out what was the significant difference between them and the children who were not in gifted programs. The one common thread among each student's upbringing was that their parents talked to them from birth, as if adults, and discussed everything with them. In some cases, the parents exposed them to math concepts, books, writing, drawing, science, the arts, music, athletics, crafts, vocational skills, and hundreds of other skills. Whatever the child was exposed to in infancy and their toddler years, they already showed talent and ability even in kindergarten, first, second, and third grades. Also, giftedness spans a wide range of talent—for some it may be scoring high on a test of verbal abilities, for others it may be nonverbal abilities, and for many it could be gifted in art, music, sports, or a hobby. The early exposure to develop the brain networks for a particular talent grows those neuron connections to cause someone to excel in a particular area. It confirmed for me the fact that whatever we expose a child to he or she will learn. I founded National Reading Diagnostics Institute to teach accelerated learning to help learners improve in memory, reading comprehension, listening comprehension, study skills, note taking, and test-taking skills. I have consistently seen children from pre-school, kindergarten, and first grade through twelfth grade, college, and adults accelerate their reading and math abilities by an average of two to five years growth in as short a time as two to eight months. Anyone *can* learn how to learn anything quickly by using the accelerated plan provided. If we teach young people how to learn in an accelerated way, we will see a nation of students who are ready for higher-level work at earlier ages, instead of finding upper grade students and adults dropping out of society because no one has taught them *how* to learn.

Just as young people can be trained in the methods of accelerated learning, so can mature citizens. Studies have shown that our brain does not decline after retirement.

We have sentenced millions of people in their 70s, 80s, 90s, and 100s or older into believing that their days of learning are over. You read earlier in the book that increased stimulation from our senses to the brain causes the development of our nerve cells and their interconnections necessary for continued brain growth and development. That development continues all through our life. It is society that promotes the false belief that our development is over when we retire. A study was conducted by the National Institute of Aging on ninety- and hundred-year old nuns in Mankato, Minnesota. Hundreds of them had donated their brains to research after they died to see whether the stimulation of their mind with mental exercise caused their brain cells to branch out, adding more connections between brain cells. Those nuns continued to learn and developed their minds and did not seem to suffer from dementia, Alzheimer's and other debilitating brain diseases as early or as severely as the general population. (from Building a Better Brain, by Daniel Golden, *National Geographic,* June 1994, p. 63-70.)

We do not have to stop learning when we graduate school, or when we retire. Learning can be a lifelong pursuit, bringing with it new skills, new interests, new hobbies, new talents, and new contributions to the lives of people around us and the world. We can choose to take continuing education courses from others and can master them in an accelerated way, or we can plan an accelerated program of self-study using the tools in this book. Live each day as if a new life is ahead of us. Age is an illusion. Decide to wake up each day as fresh and vibrant as you did as a child, teen, or young adult, looking forward to your entire life ahead of you. Many talented and gifted writers, scientists, artists, inventors, musicians, and craftspeople began their careers after sixty or seventy! You can, too!

Teaching Others

One of the best ways to learn a subject is to teach it to others. To teach, you must digest the subject, make it a part of you, and then express it in your own ways to others. By doing so, you become familiar with the subject and, over time, even become an expert in the subject. Take the subject you have studied and try to teach it to someone else. It does not have to be formal instruction. You can share what you learned with a family member, a friend, a child, or a co-worker who is interested in the same subject. Find out their superlinks learning style and brain style and teach it to them in their best style.

You can even share the knowledge you gained in this book with someone. People love to hear about themselves. Share the knowledge you gained about superlinks learning styles and brain styles and accelerated learning with friends, family, and co-workers as a way to reinforce in your mind what you have learned. This will help make the information a lasting part of yourself as well.

Transforming Yourself and the World

You have invested time in reading this book and working through it. Now that you have completed this book and the area of study you used as an example to learn these techniques, you have that time freed up so you can put what you learned to use. You can apply these techniques to learn any other field you wish to learn. Can you help yourself with that knowledge? Can you help someone else? Can you use it at your job? Can you use it to help your family? Can you use it to solve a problem in your community, nation, or the world? Can you use it to help students in schools, colleges, or any educational institution?

Exercise: Think about the subject you chose to learn as you worked through this book. List all the ways that you can apply what you learned to your daily life, using what you learned for your personal transformation, to help others, or to transform the world.

Take Action for Your Own Personal Transformation, the Attainment of Your Dreams, and Making the World a Better Place

It is time that we move out of the dark ages and into the age of enlightenment of how to learn in an accelerated way to keep pace with the times. By knowing the tools for how to learn anything quickly, you will be able to apply the skills and knowledge much quicker to achieve your own personal transformation and in transforming the world. Applying what you learned can lead to your personal transformation and the attainment of your dreams.

APPENDIX

How to Use Your Superlinks Learning Style and Brain Style to Improve Reading Comprehension in Different Fields of Learning

As one embarks on one's lifelong learning plan, one may encounter a variety of fields that one must learn. This section provides sample applications of how to use your superlinks learning style and brain style to improve reading comprehension to master different fields of learning. These sample applications provide examples to improve reading comprehension to help you apply what you learned about your superlink and accelerated learning to master different subjects.

The sample applications are in the following fields: math, writing, technical reading (computer manuals), the sciences, sports, and vocational fields and hobbies. For each subject, adaptations for each superlinks learning style and brain style are provided giving you comprehension strategies to boost your brain power and use it to accelerate your learning in that field.

Application of Superlinks Learning Styles and Brain Styles to Improve Comprehension for Learning How to Learn Math

Math is used in all segments of society. It is used for business, for home and personal use, for school and college courses in math, or use of math in other fields such as science, economics, history, computer science, health, nutrition, art, music, or vocational fields. We can use our superlink learning

252

style and brain style to improve comprehension for accelerating our ability to learn how to learn math. The following are some basic adaptations to use for learning any field of math using our superlink.

Visual Left Brain: See the numbers and problem. Needs to read directions written out in words in a step-by- step way. Comprehends best the steps to solving the problem if they can be read with a written description accompanying the numerical steps.

Visual Right Brain: See the numbers and the problem in its entirety with the answer. It must be accompanied by graphic illustration in color to demonstrate the problem. The graphics can be in the form of pictures, charts, diagrams, photographs, or real objects. Several examples of the same type of problem, complete with the answers need to be seen so the right side of the brain can see the understand it.

Auditory Left Brain: Must verbally talk through the problem in a step-by-step way. Needs a verbal explanation of each step and how to do the problem.

Auditory Right Brain: Must see the numbers and the problem with accompanying pictorial, real-life examples, written out in a global way, complete with the answers, and then talk through the problem using sensory language. The use of music and sound can accompany the illustration. Needs to talk through and see with pictorial examples several samples of the same type of problem with the answers to understand the pattern of how it is done.

Tactile Left Brain: Write down the numbers and the problem in a step-by-step way. Must write the written explanations or directions to doing the problem. Use hands-on manipulatives to accompany the written directions. Relate the problems to feelings. Needs to work with someone they like.

Tactile Right Brain: Need to write out the numbers and whole problem with the answers accompanied by drawing or sketches in color to illustrate the problem. Needs to use hands-on manipulatives to accompany the written problem. Need to write out several samples of the same type of problem with the answers to understand the pattern of how it is done. Need to connect feeling to the story problem. Need to work with people they like.

Kinesthetic Left Brain: Physically act out story problem using concrete real-life examples in a game, simulation, or role-play in a step-by-step way and talk about it. Write the numbers in large size while standing up at a board or flip chart, and talk through the problem in a step-by-step way. Use sports or game equipment or physical exercise or movement as a bonus for working out each problem to keep actively engaged while doing the math.

Kinesthetic Right Brain: Physically act out the story problem with concrete, real-life examples in a global way with the answer. Do several examples of the same type of problem with the answers so the right side of the brain can understand the pattern of how to do it. Use large manipulatives to illustrate the problem. Write the numbers and the problem in large-size while standing up at a board or flip chart. Play sports, games, or do a physical activity while practicing the math problem. Keep the body physically engaged during the process of working the problems.

Application of Superlinks Learning Styles and Brain Styles to Learn How to Learn and Improve Writing Skills

Good writing is essential for communication, whether it is for business, essays and research for schools and colleges, personal communication, or for technical writing for computer programs or instruction manuals. We can use our superlinks learning style and brain style to improve comprehension to learn how to improve writing skills.

Visual Left Brain: Plan your writing using a left-brain outline. Use a graphic organizer or outline in a step-by-step way to see all the parts of the planned written piece before attempting to write. The organizer should contain a checklist to go over to make sure all components essential for good writing have been included. Here is an example of a graphic organizer to improve writing:

Title: _____

I: Main Idea
  A-Details
  B-Details
    1-Examples
    2-Examples

II-Main Idea
   A-Details
     1-Examples
     2-Examples
   B-Details

After writing the piece, go through an evaluative checklist to make sure the following items have been covered:

Evaluative Checklist for Good Writing
Focus or topic:
- Do I have a focus or topic for this piece?
- Do I stay on the topic consistently?
- Does each paragraph have a main idea?

Details and examples to support the topic:
- Do I have details to support the main idea?
- Do I use examples to illustrate the details?
- Are the details and examples clear and understandable?

Logical organization:
- Do I write in paragraph form?
- Does each paragraph have a main idea (either stated or inferred) supported by details and examples that relate to the main idea?
- Is the order in which the paragraphs, and sentences within the paragraphs, logical?
- Do I use transition words between paragraphs, or within paragraphs, to make connections between thoughts clear?
- Do I have a good introduction?
- Do I have a good closing?

Mechanics:

- Do I use complete sentences?
- Do I vary the types of sentence types to make the piece more interesting to read?
- Do I have good sentence structure?
- Are the sentences grammatical?
- Do I use correct capitalization, punctuation, and spelling?
- Do I have correct word usage?
- Did I proofread for repetition or omitted words?
- Is it legible?

Keeping a chart with this checklist for the visual left-brain learner helps them to see whether their piece is organized. They can check off each skill item as they go through it so they can see what they have done correctly and on what they need to do more work.

Visual Right Brain: Needs to draw a mind map of the piece as a plan before doing the actual writing. Must see the plan drawn out first. Example:

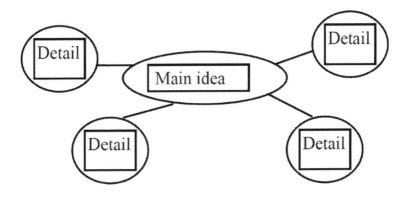

After writing the piece following the mind map, make the

Evaluative Checklist for Good Writing into a mind map form of the points to go over to evaluate the piece to make sure all components are included. Further elaboration on each of the evaluative checklist areas as described for the Visual Left-Brain learner can be added. This format helps the visual right-brain person see graphically what they need to include in a written piece.

Auditory Left Brain: Use the left-brain outline from the Evaluative Checklist for Good Writing as described above in the Visual Left Brain Learner section, but talk through each part aloud. After writing the piece, read aloud each portion of the checklist to evaluate the written piece. Reread the written piece aloud to see if the components in the evaluative checklist have been covered.

Auditory Right Brain: Turn the Evaluative Checklist for Good Writing into a right-brain mind map as described in the Visual Right Brain section for writing above, but talk through each part aloud. After writing the piece, read aloud each portion of the mind map checklist to evaluate the piece. Reread the written piece aloud to see if the components in the evaluative checklist have been covered.

Tactile Left Brain: Write the outline for a written piece using the left-brain outline format of the Evaluative Checklist for Good Writing as described in the Visual Right Brain section above. Relate the piece to your feelings. After writing the piece, write the components of the evaluative checklist and place a check mark for each item that the piece contains. Rewrite the written piece to include any of the missing components.

Tactile Right Brain: Plan the written piece by writing the Evaluative Checklist for Good Writing into a right-brain mind map format as described in the Visual Right Brain section above, filling in each bubble with the topics, subtopics, and examples. Relate the piece to your own feelings. After writing the piece using the mind map plan, evaluate it using the mind map checklist. Highlight or underline in color the portions that need reworking. Rewrite those portions until all components have been included in the written piece.

Kinesthetic Left Brain: Plan out the piece by making the left-brain outline format of the Evaluative Checklist for Good Writing as described in the Visual Left Brain section above by standing up and writing the outline on a flip chart or white board. In your mind, visualize yourself doing the actions involved in each portion of the story. Physically act out or role play what you want to write about if it is possible. After writing the piece, mount the evaluative checklist for writing on a board. Stand up and read aloud your piece, using your large arm muscles to check off each item on the checklist that you have covered. Rewrite the piece to see that all components are covered.

Kinesthetic Right Brain: Make a right-brain mind map of the Evaluative Checklist for Good Writing as described in the Visual Right Brain section above by standing up and writing on a flip chart or white board. In your mind, visualize yourself doing the actions involved in each portion of the story. Physically act out or role play what you want to write about if it is possible. After writing the piece, mount the evaluative mind map checklist for writing on a board. Stand up and read aloud your piece, using your large arm muscles to check off each item on the checklist that you have covered. Rewrite the piece to see that all components are covered. Reward yourself each time as another area of the checklist is completed, by doing something you like or doing a sports move.

Application of Superlinks Learning Stylesand Brain Stylesto Learn to Improve Reading Comprehension to Learn How to Learn Technical Reading

Driving the information highway or surfing the Internet requires ability in the field of technical reading. Technical reading has become an important area that does not receive much attention in reading programs. It is needed to read data on your computer screen, instructional manuals, computer manuals, and directions for using everyday technological equipment, such as cameras, microwaves, DVDs, putting together furniture, or installing a software program. Below are adaptations to help you use your superlinks learning style and brain style to improve reading comprehension to learn how to learn and master technical reading.

Visual Left Brain: Technical reading is easy for you to understand. Seeing words, ideas, and numbers written in step-by-step way comes easy for you. Since this is the general format of technical material, it is compatible to this superlink.

Visual Right Brain: You will need to see graphic illustrations to accompany the technical readings. Graphs, charts, diagrams, drawings, photographs, or real-life examples are a must for you in order to understand the reading. If there are none, you will need to do experiential visual right-brain reading comprehension, taking each sentence, and converting it into a drawing or illustration. Since you have a hard time following the step-by-step directions involved in technical reading, you need to read through the introduction and the summary of the technical manual and look at all the topics and headings first to get an overview of what the manual contains. Make a schematic diagram in a mind map form of the topics first, and then as you read, fill in the detail bubbles connected with each topic so you will have an overview of the entire manual. Use color to highlight different sections. Make an attractive poster or flow chart so that you can refer to the steps in the technical reading at a glance.

Auditory Left Brain: Read the technical material aloud in a step-by-step way. The technical manual is written in a left-brain way that appeals to your left brain. Reading it aloud puts it into your best mode of learning. You may wish to discuss or explain the steps to someone else so that you can hear it aloud and process it better in your brain.

Auditory Right Brain: You will need to make a mind map of the technical reading and talk about the main points. To do this, go through the introduction and conclusion of the technical reading as well as look at the headings and topics first. Include these in the mind map and then as you read the details of each, add them as bubbles connected to the main ideas. Try to enact the steps with the real objects or materials as you read. You will probably be tempted to just jump in and do the activities described in the technical reading first and then when you make a mistake, by trial and error fix it,

261

referring to the manual when necessary. If this is the case, do the trial and error first, and then go through the technical manual to refine your process and make sure you have not missed anything important to the task.

Tactile Left Brain: As you read the manual, copy down the instructions in a step-by-step way. Taking notes and the act of writing will help you to learn it. If possible, use your hands to work on the equipment or machinery being described in the instructions *as you read.* For example, if the manual describes steps to be done on the computer or on equipment, as you read each step, perform the action on the equipment. Try to involve your feelings in having a purpose that is meaningful to you in doing the task. If possible, work with someone you like as you learn it.

Tactile Right Brain: As you read the technical material, make a mind map with sketches, drawings, and diagrams of what you are learning. Use colors and designs in making the mind map. Draw a schematic diagram of what you need to do. Before beginning, get the global picture or overview of the entire process by looking at the introduction, conclusion, and main headings throughout the task. Use these as the main points in your mind map. Then fill in the details connected to the main point as you read. If possible, use your hands to work on the equipment as you go along. As you read each portion, enact the process with your hands on the actual tools or equipment. Try to involve you feelings in the process by having a motivation or reason for reading the material. If possible, work with someone you like as you learn.

Kinesthetic Left Brain: Physically do or perform the actions described in the reading in a step-by-step way as you read. Read while working on the actual equipment or tools. Make a large left-brain outline on a flip chart or board as you read, while standing up. Talk through the steps aloud as you perform them. Wherever possible, relate the material to the actual performance of the task.

Kinesthetic Right Brain: Look over the material, focusing on the introduction and the conclusion and the main headings before reading. Look at any diagrams, pictures, or charts first. As you go through the technical manual, make a large size mind map on a flip chart or large board while standing up, sketching out with pictures and key words the main points. Physically perform the task as you read for best results. You will probably want to jump right in and do it, and learn by trial and error. You can do so, but refer to the technical reading as a double check to make sure you are in the right direction.

Application of Superlinks Learning Styles and Brain Styles to Increase Reading Comprehension to Learn How to Learn and Improve in the Sciences

While each discipline has its own tradition, any subject can be adapted to be compatible with each of the superlinks learning styles and brain styles. There are many fields of sciences, but there are certain common characteristics in learning each of them: reading research of others and experimenting by forming hypotheses and testing them using the scientific method. These processes can be adapted for each of the superlinks learning styles and brain styles so that anyone can be successful in learning and improving reading comprehension in learning how to learn the sciences.

Visual Left Brain: Read the data or research in a printed form. For experiments, follow step-by-step directions as written in books or printed in charts. Keep written charts of your experiments in an organized way.

Visual Right Brain: Look at illustrations, pictures, diagrams, photographs, or watch live demonstrations. Use texts that are accompanied by graphic illustrations. In performing experiments, use pictorial charts and diagrams or flow charts of the tasks. Icons and symbols will help you see at a glance the steps you need to perform. Look at the whole picture of the task before beginning so that you can see the sequential steps in its larger context. Color code equipment or graphs to help you follow steps in order. If possible, watch someone do the experiment so you have a visual model of what needs to be done.

Auditory Left Brain: Read the research aloud and discuss it with others. Talk through the steps of an experiment first and as you do it. Try to work with others so you can discuss your ideas as you work. Use a voice recorder to record your results as you go along and play it back to think through the experiment.

Auditory Right Brain: You will need to make a mind map of the scientific readings putting down the key points. Get a global overview of the entire process first before beginning. To do this, go through the introduction and conclusion of the science reading as well as look at the headings and topics first. Talk about the main points, preferably with others. Talk through the experiment as you do it. Enact the steps with the real objects or materials. If you have someone to talk to as you do the experiment, it is ideal. If not, use a voice recorder to record what you do in the experiment and play it back later. You can also add musical accompaniment to your recording. You may want to jump in and do the experiment first and learn by trial and error, adjusting it as you go along.

Tactile Left Brain: As you read science material, copy down notes in a step-by-step way. You learn by the act of writing. Write your plan for your experiment in a step-by-step way first. Use your hands to do the experiment as you read your plan. Write your results in a step-by-step way. Try to involve your feelings in having a purpose that is meaningful to you in doing the task. If possible, work with someone you like as you learn it.

Tactile Right Brain: As you read science material, make a mind map with sketches, drawings, and diagrams of what you are learning. Use colors and designs in making the mind map. Draw a schematic diagram of what you need to do. Before beginning, get the global picture or overview of the entire process by looking at the introduction, conclusion, and main headings throughout the task. Use these as the main points in your mind map. Then fill in the details connected to the main point as you read. If possible, use your hands to do the experiment, rather than watch others. Before beginning an experiment, draw or sketch out what you plan to do. Make sketches, drawings, diagrams, or charts of the results of the experiment. Use color and design. Try to involve your feelings in the process. If possible, work with someone you like as you learn.

Kinesthetic Left Brain: As you read scientific material, visualize yourself sequentially doing the actions described. If possible, physically perform the actions described in the reading in a step-by-step way as you read. Read while working on the actual science equipment. Plan your experiment by making a large left-brain outline on a flip chart or board as you read, while standing up. Talk through the steps aloud as you perform them. Wherever possible, relate the material to the actual performance of the task. Keep a record of what you have done by making a large chart on a board while standing up. You will do well to work in a group setting, making it more active and lively.

Kinesthetic Right Brain: Look over the material, focusing on the introduction and the conclusion and the main headings before reading. Look at any diagrams, pictures, or charts first. As you go through the science readings, make a large size mind map on a flip chart or large board while standing up, sketching out with pictures and key words the main points. Stand up to draw or sketch out your plan for the experiment. Use color, symbols, and icons wherever possible. Do the experiment and record the results in a mind map on a flip chart, with sketches. You will probably want to jump right in and do it, and learn by trial and error. You can do so, but double check to make sure you are working in the right direction. You will do well to work in a group setting, making it more active and lively.

Application of Superlinks Learning Styles and Brain Styles
to Improve Reading Comprehension to Learn How to Learn
Sports or Dancing

Some people seem to take naturally to sports or dance. They just seem to pick these up with natural ease. Sports and dance are other areas that can be best learned if adapted to one's natural style of learning. People of all superlinks learning styles and brain styles can improve reading comprehension to learn how to learn and master sports or dancing if instruction is compatible with the way their brain thinks. The following are adaptations so that people of all superlinks learning styles and brain styles can learn how to learn or improve in mastering sports and dancing.

Visual Left Brain: Read written instructions on how to perform the sport or dance. Enact each step as you read. The instructions should describe every small detail of movement required to perform the sport or dance successfully. Watch yourself in a mirror so you can check your performance against the model.

Visual Right Brain: Look at illustrations, pictures, diagrams, photographs, or watch live demonstrations of the sport or dance. First see the entire process, before going into each step. Find illustrations that show pictorially each movement of the sport or dance. Photographs are better than videos or DVDs unless you stop the action of each video or DVD so you can get a clear view of each step. Watch yourself in a mirror so you can check your performance against the model. You can also videotape yourself performing and compare it to the model.

Auditory Left Brain: You need to hear each step of the direction verbally. Then talk through the steps as you do them. Make sure it is broken down into every single movement you are required to do. For example, Put your left foot forward six inches. Lift the heel of your right foot. Try to work with others so you can discuss the steps and movements. Make an audio recording of the instructions given by others so you can play it back again and again until you comprehend them.

Auditory Right Brain: Observe someone performing the entire sport or dance, getting a global overview of the process. Have them describe a few key movements using few sensory words. Make an audio recording of these instructions so you can play them back. Turn the music on and jump in and do it, getting it by trial and error. Talk through the key points of the steps with someone. Have someone observe you and tell you in a few simple sensory words how to adjust your performance.

Tactile Left Brain: In a step-by-step way, write down the instructions that you read, hear, or observe for the movements you will have to do. Make sure you write each detailed movement your body will have to do. Then enact each step with your body, following your written notes. Get your feelings involved in the sport or dance. Try to work with someone you like as you learn.

Tactile Right Brain: Watch someone do the entire process of the sport or dance first. Then make sketches or drawings of the movements you will have to do. Follow your drawings as you perform the movement. Try to involve your feelings in the process. Use music that you like to help you move. If possible, work with someone you like as you learn the sport or dance.

Kinesthetic Left Brain: Join in with others who are performing the sport or dance and follow along in a step-by-step way. Have a coach guide you through it, giving you step-by-step verbal directions and carry it out as you listen. Your kinesthetic sense will get an automatic feel for the movements and it will come easily and naturally for you. You can pick it up just by working with others who are performing it in a step-by-step way.

Kinesthetic Right Brain: You will learn it by just jumping in and doing the sport or dance with others. Observe the entire process first so you have the big picture or overview. Then just get involved by doing it. Learning a sport or dance by doing it comes easily for you. By participating, you learn by trial and error. A coach can guide you where you need refinement. The action and movement of the sports and dance, and the fun of competition, makes this an easy area for you to master.

Application of Superlinks Learning Styles and Brain Styles to Improve Reading Comprehension to Learn How to Learn Vocational Fields and Hobbies

There are numerous vocational fields and hobbies in which people are engaged for work and play. These involve learning a skill that needs to be performed. This area range encompasses construction; architecture; designing; landscaping; interior decoration; plumbing; electrical engineering; painting; wallpapering; gardening; agriculture;

farming; carpentry; building airplanes, trucks, or cars; delivery; driving; trucking; shipping; sales; marketing; crafts; textiles; sewing; knitting; fashion designing; jewelry making; modeling; art; music; machine repairs; restaurant and food industry; entertainment; and numerous other fields. Learning any of these fields can become easy and quicker if the instruction is adapted to our superlinks learning styles and brain styles. The following are adaptations to improve reading comprehension to learn how to learn any vocational field or hobby through your superlinks learning style and brain style.

Visual Left Brain: Read written instructions on how to perform the task. Enact each step as you read. The instructions should describe every small detail of movement required to perform the task successfully.

Visual Right Brain: Look at illustrations, pictures, diagrams, photographs, or watch live demonstrations of the task. First see the entire process, before going into each step. Find illustrations that show pictorially each movement of the job. Photographs are better than videos unless you stop the action of each video so you can get a clear view of each step.

Auditory Left Brain: You need to hear each step of the direction verbally. Then talk through the steps as you do them. Make sure it is broken down into every single movement you are required to do. Try to work with others so you can discuss the steps of the task. Make an audio recording of the instructions given by others so you can play them back again and again until you comprehend them.

Auditory Right Brain: Observe someone performing the entire task, getting a global overview of the process. Have them describe a few key movements using few sensory words. Make an audio recording these instructions so you can play them back. You can add musical accompaniment, if you like. Jump in and do it, getting it by trial and error. If you wish, you can work with music playing in the background. Talk through the key points of the steps with someone. Have someone observe you and tell you in a few simple sensory words how to adjust your performance of the task.

Tactile Left Brain: In a step-by-step way write down the instructions that you read, hear, or observe for the task you will have to do. Make sure you write each detailed step. Then enact each step, following your written notes. Get your feelings involved in the job. Try to work with someone you like as you learn.

Tactile Right Brain: Watch someone do the entire process of the task first. Then make sketches or drawings of the job you will have to do. Follow your drawings as you perform the task. Try to involve your feelings in the process. Use music that you like to help you move. If possible, work with someone you like as you learn the job.

Kinesthetic Left Brain: Join in with others who are performing the task and follow along in a step-by-step way. Have a coach guide you through it, giving you step-by-step verbal directions and carry them out as you listen. Your kinesthetic sense will get an automatic feel for the job and it will come easily and naturally for you. You can pick it up just by working with others who are performing it in a step-by-step way.

Kinesthetic Right Brain: You will learn it by just jumping in and doing the task with others. Observe the entire process first so you have the big picture or overview. Then just get involved by doing it. Learning by doing comes easily for you. By participating, you learn by trial and error. A coach can guide you where you need refinement. The action and movement of a skill or task makes this easy for you to learn.

BONUS FOR READERS

How To Find Your Fastest Way To Improve Reading Comprehension: How To Take The Superlinks Learning Style Inventory Test: Linksman Learning Style Preference Assessment™ And Linksman Brain Hemispheric Preference Assessment™

If you wish to take the Superlinks Learning Style and Brain Style Inventory, consisting of the Linksman Learning Style Preference Assessment™ and Linksman Brain Hemispheric Preference Assessments,™ a simple, quick online learning style and brain style assessment inventory that is automatically scored, giving instant results in a personalized report, you can go to any of the following three websites: www.superlinkslearning.com or www.readinginstruction.com, or www.keystoreadingsuccess.com which is the accelerated program of K-12, college and adult reading, memory, note taking, study, and test-taking skills. The Superlinks assessment is the same whether taken through any of these three Internet sites. There is an English and Spanish version of the tests, with more languages in the works. The assessment on the Keys to Reading Success™ website also contains a pre-K, kindergarten, Grade 1 through Grade 12, college, and adult reading diagnostic test, instantly scored with a prescriptive reading plan to accelerate learning, plus lessons to improve reading comprehension, memory, study skills, phonics, fluency, vocabulary, and test-taking for reading in any content area subject through each of the brain's eight superlinks learning styles and brain styles or your fastest way of learning. Lessons have adaptations for all superlinks learning styles and brain hemispheric preference styles. It contains an entire reading comprehension, memory, study, and test-taking skills curriculum for any age, whether for pre-K, kindergarten, Grade 1 through Grade 12, college, or adult, in each of the superlinks learning styles and brain hemispheric preference styles.

Once you take the superlinks learning style and brain style test, you will get your results and a detailed report on how you learn the best, what materials you need, what is the best learning environment, what are the best learning strategies, and how you best communicate with others and want others to communicate with you.

Find Your Own and Other's Fastest and Best Way of Learning to Improve Reading Comprehension and Learning

You can go to the website to get a license to take the online version of the Superlinks assessment. **Note:** Use the special discount code provided to the readers of this book *How to Improve Reading Comprehension Quickly by Knowing Yu Personal Reading Comprehension Style: Quick, Easy Tips to Improve Comprehension through the Brain's Fastest Superlinks Learning Style.* The discount will give you access to the test at a nominal fee from the usual cost for the test. To access a license to take the test, go to: http://www.readinginstruction.com and select from the Explore Learning Store: Superlinks to Accelerated Learning™ Assessment and enter the discount code: **HTLAQ** or contact info@keyslearning.com. You can also access the test through www.keystoreadingsuccess.com or www.superlinkslearning.com and apply the same discount code.

If you are a teacher, parent, coach, trainer, sports coach, employer, or someone who wishes to have students, trainees, employees, athletes, or group members take the test, you can get bulk licenses at special rates by contacting info@keyslearning.com.

It will score the results for you instantly and automatically and give you an instant personalized report of your best superlink. From there, go to the chapter that describes your superlinks learning style and brain style to begin using the revolutionary brain-based approach for learning any subject—fast.

ABOUT THE AUTHOR, RICKI LINKSMAN

Ricki Linksman is the author and developer of one of the fastest brain-based reading comprehension improvement, accelerated learning, learn to read, improve reading comprehension, and learn anything quickly program in the world today. She is the author of many books, including *How to Learn Anything Quickly: Quick, Easy Tips to Improve Memory, Reading, Comprehension, Test-Taking, and Learning through the Brain's Fastest Superlinks Learning Style* (previously published by Barnes and Noble and now available as an Amazon kindle eBook and physical book), *The Fine Line between ADHD and Kinesthetic Learners: 197 Kinesthetic Activities to Quickly Improve Reading, Memory, and Learning in Just 10 Weeks: The Ultimate Parent Handbook for ADHD, ADD, and Kinesthetic Learners, Your Child Can Be a Great Reader*, and *Solving Your Child's Reading Problems*, featured in *Publisher's Weekly, Women's World, Family Life, Chicago Parent, Chicago Tribune, Los Angeles Parent, San Diego Parent*, the *Naperville Sun*, and the *Lisle Sun*. She has written numerous other books on accelerated learning and reading comprehension.

Ricki Linksman is also the founder-director of National Reading Diagnostics Institute, headquartered in Naperville, Illinois, near Chicago, a training institution to help people of all ages accelerate learning and improve their reading comprehension through Superlinks™ a system she developed using neuroscience and brain research, learning styles, and brain styles. Through Ricki Linksman's methods, people can improve their performance on their job and in their studies. By improving comprehension and memory of what they read, people can excel in any field. She runs a training institution in which trainers, sports and life coaches, instructors, administrators, employers, and teachers in any field can learn how to be more effective in training employees, students, and trainees.

She also directs a parent center in which she offers reading diagnostic testing and learning style and brain style inventory assessments to find one's fastest way of learning. Through diagnostic testing her methods include developing an individual prescriptive plan followed by coaching, teaching, and tutoring students from pre-K, kindergarten, Grades 1 through Grades 12, college, to adult learners. Students show dramatic improvement whether they are in regular education, special education, Title 1, remedial reading, have ADHD or ADD, are in bilingual or ESOL, ELL, ESL, or dual language programs, or who are gifted. She was the developer of one of the first parent involvement programs in the country, and was featured in Cendant and Davidson's Reading Blaster™ 9-12 popular software program as creating a Parent Tips guidebook, and has chosen as one of the best reading experts in the country to consult in the production of Cendant's *Learn to Read*™ software package.

At National Reading Diagnostics Institute, parents are trained how to accelerate their children or teens' learning. Her Keys to Reading Success™ program includes parent involvement worksheets to help parents be more effective in providing homework help.

Ricki has been serving students in public and private schools throughout the country and around the world.

Whenever she has set up the system of accelerated learning and accelerated reading in schools, those schools have raised test scores and achievement through her methods within less than one school year. Test scores raised include CTBS, SAT, ACT, and ISAT (Illinois State Achievement Test). Her program has also been used to prepare students for career examinations in diverse fields, such as medicine and law.

Ricki Linksman is also the developer of *Keys to Reading Success*⊠, an Internet-based pre-K, kindergarten, grades 1 through 12, and college reading program to use accelerated learning techniques and learning styles and brain hemispheric preference strategies to teach students to learn to read or improve reading within four to eight months or less. The average success rate is 98-99% of all K-12 students using the program rise 2-5 grade levels in reading in 6-8 months, including students in regular education, special education, ELL, ESL, ESOL, bi-lingual and dual language, Title 1 or Remedial Reading, and gifted programs (and those with ADD or ADHD). Rusty Acree, a retired veteran and current football referee, of Richmond, Virginia, is one of many parents and grandparents who have seen the effectiveness of the program on his grandson. His grandson, who had been previously labeled with ADHD, had been left back in kindergarten for two years, yet still could neither recognize the letters of the alphabet nor read a word. When he was diagnosed by Ricki as a kinesthetic right-brain learner and was taught how to read through his kinesthetic right-brain Superlinks style he was able to learn the letters of the alphabet and could read his first book ever within 2 days. Rusty Acree who continued to see the phenomenal growth of his grandson over the next year to get to grade level in reading has called Ricki Linksman, The Michael Jordan of Reading.

Ricki developed the *Superlinks to Accelerated Learning*⊠ program with its *Linksman Learning Style Preference Assessment and Brain Hemispheric Preference Assessment*⊠, used to discover a person's best Superlink (learning style and brain style) to accelerate learning.

Her programs Keys to Reading Success™ and Superlinks to Accelerated Learning™ were selected by a foundation, the Cotchery Foundation, started by New York Jets football running back, Jericho Cotchery and his wife Mercedes Cotchery, to assist an elementary school in North Carolina raise its reading scores and is featured on the Cotchery Foundation website.

Her award-winning phonics program has been selected for use as the phonics curriculum used by Huntington™ Learning Centers throughout the country. Other companies that have used her Superlinks to Accelerated Learning™ programs include Kaplan On-line University; MFS Investment Management, Boston, a large Massachusetts financial institution who used Ricki Linksman's accelerated learning techniques to help trainers teach clients about mutual funds sales; and by one of the largest technology company in the world.

Recently, Ricki Linksman created a phonics program specially designed for kinesthetic and tactile learners, but can be used with visual and auditory learners also, including those with a right-brain or left-brain preference, called Off the Wall Phonics™. It allows students to learn to master every phonics patterns in the English language to move someone from beginning reading to college-level word reading ability within 10 game levels, of 10 games each. If followed, any student can raise their word-reading level, which can help their reading comprehension, by playing one game level per week for ten weeks, and studies have proven the average raise in word-reading level to be two to five grade levels in reading in that time.

A university football team used Keys to Reading Success™ and Superlinks to Accelerated Learning™ to improve football performance through learning styles and brain styles, helping them to their first winning season. It dramatically changed the way football coaches taught the football play book to the athletes.

She has worked as a consultant to golf instructors to improve teaching of golf through Superlinks to Accelerated Learning™ learning styles. She was a consultant to a former White Sox baseball player on product development of a pitching aid to improve pitching skills using Superlinks to Accelerated Learning™ As a trainer of trainers she has improved the effectiveness of trainers to help them reach all participants of different learning styles.

Africa from elementary school to a college, including Learning Identity, Clifton Preparatory School, and Hilton College, have adopted Keys to Reading Success and Superlinks to Accelerated Learning to improve reading.

Ricki works as a consultant to businesses, companies, and educational institutions to help people accelerate and improve learning in any field. She has done trainings for college professors and instructors at colleges and universities. She has also done volunteer work training tutors for Literacy Volunteers for America. She trained facilitators for youth outreach programs sponsored by a local police station and worked with students from DCFS (Department of Children and Family Services). She has also served as a reading expert for a pro-bono court case for a major Chicago law firm. Public schools often call on Ricki Linksman's expertise on case study teams for students.

She has run Administrator Academies in Illinois on District Reading Improvement, training superintendents and principals in steps to improve their district reading programs and scores. She has been one of the trainers for Illinois's ISAT (Illinois State Achievement Test) reading and writing tests and has trained teachers in how to raise test scores on this state test. She was one of Illinois's state validators for the Right to Reading Initiative. She has presented to many Regional Offices of Education to train teachers and administrators from many school districts in these methods.

She gives seminars and workshops, appears at book-signings, and speaks at conferences. She has presented her reading programs to tens of thousands of teachers across the country. She works as a consultant and trainer for public school districts and schools in accelerated learning techniques, raising district reading scores, and improving student achievement. She received a certificate of merit from the IASCD (Illinois Association for Supervision and Curriculum) 1999 Winn's Research Award for Maximizing School Reading Scores.

She receives thousands of letters and emails from teachers, administrators, parents, college professors, consultants, and students from all over the world who have read her books and write to her for advice on improving reading and learning performance. Her works are cited on numerous Internet sites listing excellent resources for parents and teachers, including *Conde Nast.*

She has taught graduate education courses in reading, and

another on inclusion: differentiated learning to teach to all learners through learning styles. Specializing in accelerated learning with application to reading, she has taught these techniques to students of all ages and to adults.

For parents and teachers, she has numerous books, EBooks, courses, online e-courses, podcasts, webinars, teleseminars, coaching, and consulting to accelerate learning for all types of learners, including kinesthetic, tactile, auditory, visual, with either a right-brain or left-brain preference. These materials have helped children and teens from pre-K, kindergarten, grade 1-12, and college, whether in regular education, special education, gifted, ESOL, ELL, ESL, bilingual or dual language, or Title 1 or Reading Remedial programs, or those who have ADHD or ADD.

CONTACT INFORMATION

Ricki Linksman can be contacted at:
National Reading Diagnostics Institute and Keys Learning,
Naperville, Illinois;

Email: info@keyslearning.com

Web sites:
http://www.readinginstruction.com
http://www.keyslearning.com
http://www.keystoreadingsuccess.com
http://www.superlinkslearning.com
http://www.nationalreadingdiagnosticsinstitute.com
http://www.offthewallphonics.com

A SPECIAL GIFT FOR READERS

The author has a special gift for readers of this book, *How to Learn Anything Quickly*:

If you would like to find your superlinks learning style and brain hemispheric preference style, or that of your family, friends, and others, as a special reader of *How to Learn Anything Quickly*, here is your special discount code to access the test at a significant discount. Go to http://www.readinginstructiom.com and from the Explore Learning Store, select Superlinks to Accelerated Learning™ Assessment and enter the discount code: **HTLAQ**.

You can also access the assessment at:
http://www.keystoreadingsuccess.com
and
http://www.superlinkslearning.com
and apply the same discount code.

Note: When you get to the order page, scroll down to enter your discount code where the discounted price will appear. After taking the test, it will instantly be scored and give you a personalized report on your best superlink learning style and brain style with tips on how to learn anything quickly. You can return to the matching chapter in this book to read about how you can learn quickly through your superlinks learning style and brain style and improve your own or others' memory, reading, comprehension, note taking, study, test-taking skills, and learning. Enjoy the rewards of personal transformation!